TESTIMONIALS

Trust is one of the single most important predictors of positive and productive relationships and organisations. There are almost one million research papers published about trust in leadership, more than two million research papers looking at trust and management and almost 2.5 million research papers about trust in organisations, which underpins the importance of this subject.

Melanie Marshall's book cuts through but is based on this mass of research and offers practical ideas and principles to help build trust in organisations and teams whilst being easy to read and powerful. This is an important subject, and this book deserves to be read in every organisation.

– Dr David Wilkinson, Editor-in-Chief, The Oxford Review.

If a person was to pick up this book and think they were going to receive a clear cut, textbook definition of what is trust, then they would be mistaken.

But what the reader will gain is an abundance of practical gems that will get them thinking, reflecting, and hopefully changing their behaviour – all towards the goal of cultivating TRUST!

The conversational, deeply researched, sometimes witty and honest style of Melanie's writing has impact. Even if you only read the pop-outs, you will get something rich from this book.

– Jacqui Parle, Director, Consulting Services,
BPA Analytics Pty Ltd.

When trust in our economy erodes, we know what happens – downturns and recessions. Melanie Marshall shows us something we sometimes overlook – without a climate of trust in our workplaces, our organisations face similarly bad outcomes.

This book will help you understand that withholding trust, or waiting for others to show it first, is the path to downturn in the culture of a workplace. Melanie is a wise guide in helping us to appreciate the skills, methods and thinking that will allow us to step up and build the economy of trust we need in our workplaces, our organisations, and our lives.

– Tony Hewson, Organisational Behaviour and Culture Change Executive, Royal Australian Air Force.

I was enthralled within the first few pages. Melanie has managed to capture and validate what we have all experienced. This book is for leaders, managers, and anyone who has felt the impacts of a toxic workplace. Cutting through the fog of distrust and poor organisational culture, this book offers a clear path forward.

Melanie challenges your mindset on leadership with personal and relatable stories that allow the reader to reflect on their own career and the role they play.

This is a powerful book that overturns current leadership and management thinking – providing us all hope we can do better.

– Susan Chambers, Nurse Manager.

This book is well paced and provides a well-structured path when following the HEART+SOUL approach to trust. I found the book very affirming at a personal and professional level, and really enjoyed the nuggets of wisdom. As a manager who has focused on kindness, I have been told that my management style is not forceful enough, but this book has confirmed that my focus on 'soft' skills is in fact the right path for me. Insightful leaders reading this book will understand that long-term results follow from trust, but not the other way around.

– **Tony Jamieson, Manager, Youth Justice Learning and Development, Department of Children, Youth Justice & Multicultural Affairs.**

TRUST

The foundation of healthy organisations and teams

MELANIE MARSHALL

Published by Melanie Marshall

First published in 2021 in Brisbane, Australia

Copyright © Melanie Marshall

www.melaniemarshall.com.au

Edited by Jenny Magee

Cover design by Hayley Jenkins

Typeset, printed and bound in Australia by BookPOD

ISBN: 978-0-6451508-0-3 (paperback)
ISBN: 978-0-6451508-1-0 (ebook)

NATIONAL LIBRARY OF AUSTRALIA

A catalogue record for this book is available from the National Library of Australia

CONTENTS

INTRODUCTION

Most of us want to be connected to something bigger and for our lives to have meaning and purpose. To do this, we need solid relationships with others to make us feel successful individually and as community members.

Organisations are made up of many communities, and I've been in the change and culture game long enough to know that transformation requires structural and personal effort for everyone to own their part in it.

Personal and work environments can be damaging when people aren't respected for who they are or what they offer through perspective, skills, and experience – particularly if their difference questions the status quo.

Vision statements and strategy documents are meaningless unless people's capability and wisdom are believed, strengthened and leveraged to design and deliver what the organisation promotes.

My most treasured moments are when faith in a team or individual's ability to overcome challenges and deliver what is needed gives people the permission and freedom to offer what matters most and provide services they're proud of.

TRUST

Trust is the foundation for authentic and meaningful relationships that allow us to be the best versions of ourselves. It enables us to smile, knowing that what we do has meaning and makes a difference.

With the autonomy and freedom of trust, you get stuff done. Without it, you can feel undervalued, frustrated and not good enough. One client aptly described this as being stuck in a negative infinity loop, which is soul destroying and can take considerable time to heal.

I wish I'd written this book earlier, as it would have saved much unnecessary angst. It would have also made our respective journeys more enjoyable and easier to travel.

But we're here now, and this book is dedicated to you. You deserve to be happy, productive and appreciated for who you are, what you do, and how you do it.

I also want this joy for the people we live, work, and play with because we all could benefit from more belief in ourselves and each other.

To make this happen, it's worth recognising that incremental and consistent shifts in the way we think and behave impact far beyond our immediate and secondary circles of influence.

This book will support reflection on your organisational culture and the vital role you play. We will highlight a range of personal competencies necessary for trust and offer a practical approach to apply them to yourself, your team, and your organisation.

For ease of reference, the book is in three parts:

Part 1: **Understand.** Here we set the scene, detailing the importance of trust and why it can be hard to give and receive.

Part 2: **Be.** Next, we explore the competencies of trust as a guide for who we need to be for ourselves and others.

Part 3: **Do.** The final part offers a model for action, practising the concepts so you can achieve results.

Although this is a book for organisational strength, it starts with you and how you choose to lead.

Read the book, take what is useful and make the process of building and maintaining trust your own.

With kindness,

Melanie

DISCLAIMER

In this book, the stories I share are reflections on moments in time, in the spirit of owning the lessons learned, with enduring respect and care for everyone involved or impacted. Hence, organisations and individual names have been changed to respect people's identities and privacy.

TRU

PART ONE

UNDERSTAND

CHAPTER 1

ORGANISATIONAL DISTRUST

'All leadership is a transfer of trust. It stays with no man or woman but is in a constant state of forward movement, into the future, for the best.'

– Robin Dreeke

Trust is the firm belief in the reliability, truth or strength of a person or thing. It can also be a confident expectation.[1] It is the non-negotiable element of our most valued relationships, leadership, and high performing teams.

Given that work consumes so much of our lives, we must trust the people we spend most of our days with.

Not having trust between executive and operational areas is like shouting across a canyon, expecting the others to come over, but with no understanding of why they should or the means to do so.

> Not having trust between executive and operational areas is like shouting across a canyon, expecting the others to come over, but with no understanding of why they should or the means to do so.

Many years of reforms, transformations, and change programs across the public and private industry have resulted in varying levels of success and failure, so you can't blame people for being cynical.

A special report by The Oxford Review revealed that cultural cynicism or distrust toward organisational strategy was a major factor in whether executives and managers could successfully lead and achieve desired organisational and business changes.[2]

Understanding and addressing the reasons for distrust is vital. Lack of trust between those designing the strategy and the people responsible for executing it has 'direct negative motivational impact on employees to engage in change projects and may even extend to the extent of sabotaging change programmes.'[3]

Over the years, I've witnessed firsthand this exact disengagement and sabotage of improvement efforts across multiple government departments and private industries. For example:

- Service design and reforms that suit senior executive egos and personalities create and embed siloed organisations not designed for functional needs.

- Strategic recommendations are cherry-picked to focus on and adopt quick wins because there is no faith or trust in people's ability to deliver better operational outcomes.

- Refusal to provide requested access to people, information, and resources to support business improvement. Reluctance to give a complete picture of challenges and opportunities to facilitate genuine consultation and co-design of solutions.

- Routine overuse of consultants and contractors instead of higher value leadership and management functions performed internally.

- Reporting that reflects what people want to hear rather than what needs to be heard.

The fundamental problem is that people focus on risk and choose control rather than establishing relationships and trust.

> The fundamental problem is that people focus on risk and choose control rather than establishing relationships and trust.

We'll look deeper into the challenges of trust in Chapter Three. For now, know that when we delve into the root causes, it becomes clear that people don't generally set out to create unproductive and harmful workplaces. Most have lost their way and need guidance and support to get back on track.

More personally, no one wants to be labelled unable to work

with others, or worse, be considered dishonest, self-serving, incompetent, excluding, or over-controlling. These behaviours often happen unconsciously, covertly, and slowly over time. If left unchecked, moments of distrust can become culturally and psychologically embedded.

Accepting the reality that nothing is perfect, we choose or remain in organisations because we believe and hope that what we're working on does, can, or will make a difference.

In a formal sense, there is also a contractual and assumed level of trust in organisations, as recruitment is based on the agreed value that individual contribution can provide what the business wants to achieve.

Even with the best intentions, this is often not respected when consulting companies and external resources design transformation strategies and solutions for the way forward. Intent and capability are there, but what's missing is feeling and connection to those who own the responsibility and actions.

To build trust, you need to know what's broken, who you need to partner with, what needs to be done to fix things, and how you're going to work through things together.

ORGANISATIONAL CULTURES – HEALTHY OR HARMFUL?

At different points in my career, I've been entrenched in toxic, low-trust cultures. Despite success with people committed to fully transforming how they worked and served others, we often needed a more holistic approach to establishing better relationships across the organisation or enterprise.

This was noticeably clear in one company.

A revolving office door of managers kept asking for help to address behaviours that were highly disturbing and ingrained, stemming from the top down and leaking across multiple areas. The organisation was far from healthy.

The draining nature of continually putting out spot fires and resolving conflicts was exhausting, and I questioned whether it was time to leave. I was so low that if it were financially possible to quit work, I would have.

I wanted to believe that I could make a difference, but deep down, I felt like a total fraud as the Organisational Development lead. The results of the culture survey had come in, and they were horrible. It was no surprise given the amount of intervention work the broader Human Resources team and I had been doing.

Over the twelve months prior, we'd tried raising issues and suggested solutions with the senior executive team on numerous occasions. These were also identified immediately before the survey, but other leaders and my colleagues who shared the concerns could never get traction.

Eventually, we were told that the National Office had engaged a consulting firm to create a new leadership and performance framework for middle managers. But we had no visibility of what this was or how it would resolve the issues employees and customers experienced. The shared experiences of a trusted few made it obvious that the proposed roadmap wasn't going to address the issues or causes of the toxic enterprise-wide culture.

Despite support from those who often volunteered internal services and my particular interest in partnering, we were consistently denied permission to be involved with the external consulting team.

On a personal level, I had lost my sparkle, I felt utterly undervalued, and despite a mostly brave and smiling face, had zero confidence. It was a miserable time; my head was a mess, and I began thinking that the problem was me. I began a daily and automatic ritual of questioning whether I was the right fit for work I cared about and had been been recruited for.

In privately discussing my feelings of insecurity and wanting to leave, I received multiple assurances that my experience would be missed and that I should stay. But I didn't feel it, as I'd lost hope, was burnt out, and couldn't walk the party line anymore. My work performance and mental health were suffering, and I didn't like the person I'd become.

Stepping up and leaning in

In a last attempt to turn things around, I requested a one-on-one meeting with the CEO to discuss the recent culture survey and address the findings.

Employee feedback had confirmed what my colleagues and I

already knew – that the organisation was in complete turmoil and spiralling down at a rapid pace.

The co-designed recommendations from internal subject matter experts aligned with the survey provider. There was real concern that the senior executive team's heavy focus on middle management leadership development meant they'd missed developing themselves.

A primary finding highlighted the need for leadership cohesion and trust-building between the senior executive and middle managers. The driver was a 20 per cent disconnect between employee trust in direct line managers over their trust in senior leaders. The organisation was ripe for mutiny.

Further developing middle managers was the wrong way to address the survey findings, as it ignored the incredibly positive leadership ratings given to these managers. This was in complete contrast with the senior executive team, who were not respected by most employees. From my colleagues' and my perspective, the decision to focus again on middle managers rather than respond directly to employee concerns placed the organisation and its services at even greater risk.

It was time for a one-on-one meeting with the CEO, and I was nervous. The message I needed to deliver was tough, regardless of the evidence, how prepared I was, or the support behind me.

Ouch, that hurts!

Despite what I thought was careful language and empathic

delivery of the cultural concern, the CEO's emotional response was far more than I bargained for.

Her words were something like, 'How dare you come in here and tell me what I can and can't do!' Given I was already fragile, her rage ripped through me as I struggled to hold back tears and maintain composure.

Trusted colleagues had warned me that the CEO viewed me as a young upstart. Even though I was employed as the company's organisational culture specialist, her opinion of me was far from glowing. Hence, it took much courage to put myself into such a risky position. In hindsight, I should have thought more deeply before the conversation, but I did what I thought was right at the time, based on my experience.

External consultants had been paid to provide a high-level strategy for what team members and I had successfully delivered previously to middle managers for similar organisations.

The CEO appeared not to know that the lessons we'd learnt, combined with our cultural knowledge of what did and didn't work, had already been applied to develop and support middle managers and – as the survey demonstrated – it was working.

We had worked through days, weeks, and months of conflict mediation, holding back tidal waves of a systemically toxic culture of bullying, harassment, underperformance, and unsafe work practices. In a high-pressure service organisation where someone's bad day could result in harm or death to an employee or member of the community, it was worth the effort.

As the lead mediator and coach, I'd become a go-to person for many areas, but really all I was providing was a quiet, safe space away from the crazy so they could gather their thoughts, test out ideas, and get a pep talk before going back into battle.

Every day felt like an organisational war zone. With each story entrusted to us, it became clear that the problem was not middle managers; it was the siloed and fractured relationships among the senior executive team.

After nearly two years in the organisation, coaching managers on how to move from technical roles and adapt to people leadership and management pressures, the culture at middle-manager level had improved. The evidence was validating, and it was comforting to know that our team had made a significant difference.

Unfortunately, the lack of senior executive accountability or leadership skills was significantly driving organisational culture, performance, and people's mental health into the ground. Employees could see and feel it, and now independently backed evidence (via the survey) proved that things needed to change.

Good intentions

My conversation with the CEO was in her office, and given the sensitivity, I went in alone. I felt vulnerable, knowing that by sharing an alternative perspective, I was at considerable intrinsic risk.

Yet, I hoped for clarification that the culture survey's central recommendation was addressed as a priority. I also sought direction on how to support her and the organisation more broadly.

Desperate to connect with the CEO and her executive team, I wanted to provide assurance for my colleagues and the next wave of managers and staff that would come through my office. I wanted to let them know their voices were heard, and there was a combined senior leadership commitment to change.

My expectations were embarrassingly way out of sync. The CEO was furious, and I received a significant dressing down that let me know it was none of my business. It took all my energy to manage a full range of diverging and colliding emotions through the meeting.

With all my interpersonal conflict experience put to the test, I calmly waited out the anger, and the CEO finally became more conversational and open. It was a relief when the conversation ended better than it started, but her initial response left me feeling raw and defeated, with nothing left to give.

I cried all the way home, replaying the meeting in my head, wondering whether I had been disrespectful or whether I was just on the receiving end of the CEO having a horrendous day, month, or year.

Thankfully, it was Friday, and over the weekend, I had time to lick my wounds, decompress, go for a run, and get clarity on what I needed.

To my surprise, the CEO was happy when she came into my

office mid-Monday morning announcing that she wanted me to implement a glossy high-level middle management leadership program. Sadly, it was confirmation that I had failed to deliver the message she needed to hear. I thanked her for the offer and politely told her I had resigned earlier that morning. She appeared shocked but said it was important to follow what was right for me and wished me all the best. When asked where I was going, I replied, 'I don't know, I don't have a job yet'.

It was a huge decision. As a single mum with two kids, a new mortgage, and no immediate job to go to, I was scared but had enough in the bank for a couple of months without work. I would take any other job to keep a roof overhead and food on the table. Despite my very reasonable fear, I was living my values, and at that moment, I felt like the most powerful woman alive!

With relief and a weight off my shoulders, I was thrilled to secure another role quickly. Walking away felt light, and my head was filled with the excitement of another opportunity.

Sadly, a few months later, the toxic, low-trust culture and predicted mutiny were broadcast across local television and newspapers. The CEO moved on shortly after.

My intentions were good, and overall, I believe the CEO's were too. Like all of us, she was human. I had seen her genuine care for others, but she was getting smashed across a range of fronts, and I knew she was coming from a place of real pain.

From the CEO's perspective, I was probably just another person throwing rocks at already broken windows. I wish I knew then what I know now, and I'm grateful for the reflections and lessons I've learned since.

The problem with assumptions

Heading into that fateful meeting with the CEO, I was confident because I had the trust of the people I worked with and understood the organisational context. I felt responsible for advocating for employees at a time where things were horrid for everyone.

The independent evidence and support for how the CEO and her team needed to respond to the survey findings gave credibility to the conversation. I knew my communication was well-intended, and in wanting to be part of the solution, I was also putting my hand up to share the accountability.

But in the CEO's eyes, I did not have credibility, trust or permission to discuss what I could offer her and the senior executive team. I had not prioritised the need to understand her perspective first and had provided unsolicited advice that was not wanted or respected.

In hindsight, as much as I thought my approach was good at the time, I delivered it in a way that did not first serve the very person with whom I sought a trusting relationship.

As an accountability freak, I had also fallen into the dangerous state of taking on more than my fair share of the blame. I doubted everything I knew and felt hopeless, as all my previous attempts to support the organisation strategically had failed. I had not been allowed to participate in big picture discussions or engagements, and rightly or wrongly, I had taken this very personally.

Freedom came when I realised and accepted that regardless of title, no individual is responsible for leading a cultural shift alone. Thinking otherwise is harmful.

> Regardless of title, no individual is responsible for leading a cultural shift alone. Thinking otherwise is harmful.

Thinking it's all on us is like playing a team sport and forgetting that victory or defeat are determined by the collective efforts of our teammates and the way we play together.

Sure we have individual accountabilities, but if you know you're doing the best you can with what you have, it is useful to remember the adage, 'There is no 'I' in team'.

From that experience, I took on roles in different fields, industries, and sectors, recharged my energies, checked more of my assumptions, and dropped my 'I can save the world' attitude and ego. When I did so, work became less stressful and failure less personal.

It's fair to say that if you've ever managed teams or an organisation, you've spent plenty of time de-escalating, investigating, resolving workplace conflicts, and addressing unacceptable work behaviours as part of everyday business.

These have likely ranged from the subversive sabotage of organisational change efforts, embedded bullying and harassment cultures, employees yelling and screaming at each other, physical attacks, unions threatening stop-work action, to illegal activities. Sadly, little surprises anyone who has ever worked in employee relations or as a people manager.

We all have limits, and depending on what is going on in our lives, our ability to manage our emotions and behave in ways that serve us professionally and personally can sometimes falter.

Life experience, interpersonal issues, moral and ethical boundaries, as well as contextual factors such as situational trauma, mental health, drugs, and alcohol can have a massive impact on our ability to manage what we feel and how we express it.

> When it comes to change, it's the behaviour, not the person or people, that is the problem.

In short, we can all act out in ways that aren't congruent with our values or the relationships we want with others.

When it comes to change, it's the behaviour, not the person or people, that is the problem.

Seeing through unacceptable and toxic behaviour to connect with the people behind it can be challenging and tiring work. It becomes even harder if we're personally under pressure and ultimately accountable for what is delivered.

Throughout this book, I'll offer an approach that better serves us for providing and building trust. For now, understanding the context in which you operate and considering a broader perspective will be more useful.

THE APS PICTURE

There continues to be a plethora of Whole of Government reviews, audits, and ministerial enquiries on Australian Public Service (APS) operations.

As a typical response, multiple high-level and high-cost strategic plans are developed and agreed upon. Although these can result in some change, many fail to produce meaningful, long-term benefits. This is evident when further reviews recommend the same types of solutions as those before them.

The most recent independent review of the Australian Public Service (APS)[4] stated that the APS is not ready for the significant changes and challenges Australia will face between now and 2030. Key findings reflected historical challenges in addressing known issues involving people, enabling systems, and culture.

When we think of organisational systems, we need to think, plan and act holistically across multiple domains. The foundations for working together need to be stable if we want to deliver services people can trust.

The APS Review found that:

- More than 170 purpose statements reinforced agency priorities rather than those of the broader APS

- There were fundamental failures in managing and investing in employees
- Approximately 40 per cent of APS employee time is spent on automatable tasks
- Seventy per cent of staff reported the APS as too rigid and hierarchical.

That means people aren't supported to produce quality outcomes because agencies generally haven't been designed to run in an integrated way. The impact is that the service experience of delivery teams and their customers (internal and external) can be diabolically confusing and ineffective for meeting people's most basic needs.

At the time of the review, only three in ten Australians trusted government services. The usual recommendations to 'work in partnership', 'operate efficiently' and 'live APS values'[5] were not surprising and similar to the many reviews before them.

Of considerable challenge are the multiple interpretations of what success looks like in practice.

In response, the Government announced that it aspires to provide 'A trusted APS, united in serving all Australians'.[6]

Although the recommendations appeared overly generic, it was heartening that the APS was advised to 'double the trust scores provided by the public'.[7]

We all want to trust.

It's not that APS employees don't want to deliver to organisational plans. Instead, large consulting companies often write these strategies at incredibly high levels and frequently lack any operational perspective on implementing them.

> We all want to trust.

The research is solid, and the intentions are great, but those responsible for delivery are put in positions where they:

a. Don't know where to start

b. Aren't permitted to lead or truly leverage their expertise

c. Can't break it down

d. Are working on so many initiatives that the style and pace of change are impractical, unscalable, and unsustainable.

Employee engagement

Employee engagement began in the 1990s from Professor William Khan's work, demonstrating the importance of connecting people's physical, cognitive, and emotional states with organisational goals to achieve higher levels of commitment, drive outcome-focused behaviours, and increase work performance.[8]

A common misconception in organisational practice is that engagement comes from alignment to organisational goals. But we need to be clear that it comes from meaningful work, where we're safe to be ourselves and have the energy and resources to perform at our best.[9]

Instead of focusing on what is going wrong in an organisation, it's far better to focus on what works from various fields such as psychology, human resource management, organisational development, leadership, and business integration.[10]

Since the APS review – and in approaching things more holistically and across multiple disciplines – numerous improvements have increased employee engagement, capability and agency responsiveness to community needs during natural disasters. This has been particularly so during the COVID-19 pandemic, where government agencies' responsiveness in pulling together and responding as a unified team was indeed a transformational effort.

A significantly positive side-effect of the pandemic is proof of what is possible on an international scale with connection, clarity, and commitment to a common purpose.

In Australian Government agencies, significant investment continues to streamline internal processes and improve non-crisis ways of working. It is worth noting current efforts to introduce new Enterprise Resource Planning systems to remove duplication, operate more effectively across agencies, re-invest, and re-distribute resources to where they're most needed.

My work is mostly with government clients, and I believe permanent government employees need to be supported and enabled to move beyond crisis and pandemic responses for sustainable community benefits. In improving 'business as usual' practices, it's easier to adapt to the unexpected.

Feelings of overwhelm, burnout, and failure are prevalent among APS clients committed to delivering quality services. It's also important to recognise that Whole of Government transformation work deeply challenges the already tired, and in some cases distrusting, agencies and people within.

> It's one thing to raise trust with the community, but to turn things around, relationships and support must first be built within an organisation.

It's one thing to raise trust with the community, but to turn things around, relationships and support must first be built within an organisation.

REFLECTION

Do you, and others in your circle of influence, truly feel valued as part of the organisational team?

- Why or why not?

- *If you aren't sure, read through the last employee and customer surveys. Even high-level snapshots can provide intelligence worth more detailed understanding.*

For gaps between aspired and reported organisational performance and values, what might people say behind closed doors?

Do people feel that what they do makes a difference?

- *If you don't know, it's time to build and deepen relationships to find out.*

If you were, or are, the CEO, what would people tell you if they felt they had nothing to lose?

- What would they do if they were the CEO?

Do the 'ways of working' match the espoused values and vision?

- What would your customers say?

Start asking those you serve about ways to create safe opportunities for people to share what they feel, think, and do right now.

CHAPTER 2

CULTURE IS A TEAM SPORT

When it comes to culture, there is never a single contributor to organisational success or failure.

Organisational culture brings to mind team sports and the interconnectivity of factors that determine whether people honour the code and play their best.

> When it comes to culture, there is never a single contributor to organisational success or failure.

A special 2019 report on high-performing teams by The Oxford Review sampled 59 high-quality multi-national research papers. The report defined a high-performance team as 'one that exceeds all reasonable expectations and produces extraordinary results'. Studies have shown that high-performing teams:

1. Have seamless flows of work between members
2. Pre-empt each other's thinking and actions

3. Give and receive 'tough love' via supportive and honest feedback

4. Reflect on performance

5. Have confidence with humility

6. Own adaptive and experimental mindsets that strive for mastery

7. Brief before, during and after activities and events

8. Have high levels of commitment and ownership from all members, who are responsible for their actions and the overall performance of the team

9. Trust each other to deliver.[11]

Numerous studies identify the value of external coaching to guide and transition teams into high-performance. 'No international high-performance sports, military or emergency services team would operate without some form of coach, who is tied to their success.'[12]

> Organisations are complex systems and patterns of individuals, teams, and groups who are thinking, feeling, being, and doing in their own ways.

When teams fail, and people declare something is wrong with the 'culture', there is often limited or shared understanding of precisely what this means and how to change it.

Organisations are complex systems and patterns of individuals, teams, and groups who are thinking, feeling, being, and doing in their own ways.

If you consider organisational performance as a sport, this is how the components might compare:

Team Sport	Organisational Culture
Code (e.g. soccer, rugby, netball, cricket)	Sector (e.g. private, public) Industry (e.g. community services, health, ICT, defence)
Rules of the game and the club	Legislation, law, policy
Fans and supporters	Customers and stakeholders
Referees and umpires	Executives and managers
Scorecard and competition ladder	Governance, Key Performance Indicators (KPIs), reviews and reporting
Coaches, captains, and others, in or out of the team, that players respect and choose to follow	Leaders
Players	Employees, contractors, workers
Playing field, training spaces, locker rooms	Work environments
Sporting equipment, uniforms, protective gear	Any equipment, resources, or things people need to access and complete their work
Training and development programs	Training, guides, operating procedures, professional development programs

Table 1: Culture components comparison

> Understanding how cultural components need to work together is key when designing and knowing what, who, how, and when to change.

We need to consider all these plus more complex factors, including the physical and emotional context of work, customers' dynamic needs, and the sentiments of our communities.

Understanding how cultural components need to work together is key when designing and knowing what, who, how, and when to change.

When it comes to business, if we're not delivering value, what is the point of our actions?

When people don't see, feel, or experience meaningful benefits from their work, the standard call to action becomes 'innovate or perish' – or words to that effect. I clearly remember a Chief Information Officer (CIO) offering this line as a pep-talk to employees. Perhaps it was something he had Googled for inspiration, but it plummeted like a lead balloon. The phrase was a slap in the face for staff who had been proposing change and innovation for years. Sadly, nothing they suggested ever gained traction because the CIO also wanted people to 'do their homework' and provide evidence to prove their ideas would work.

Being innovative isn't about proving ideas will work before testing and adjusting them.

Even with evidence of what is wrong, there must be wholehearted agreement that people need to do things differently, with subject matter experts to guide or support the journey. Having faith in something new and producing evidence that it will work before it does is a huge, if not ridiculous, ask. It is particularly true if the

> Being innovative isn't about proving ideas will work before testing and adjusting them.

organisation has previously tried and failed to bring a vision to life.

The CIO knew the technology, but he didn't understand the cultural system or know how to build trust with the organisation's teams and their people.

Developing trust for change is like leading the team along a steep and rocky path up the side of a mountain. A miscalculation may result in a nasty fall, but if you focus too heavily on the risk, you won't make the climb.

Evidence-based recommendations win business cases, and risks need to be understood and mitigated. But if multiple clearances are required for staff to make even minor improvements, they might not consider it worth the effort, and the status quo will continue.

A common approach to change is to deliver communications on what to do, train people on what to do differently, and include some team building or employee engagement initiatives for good measure.

Efforts to improve culture are usually around developing

resilience, emotional intelligence, teamwork, and interpersonal skills. However, in isolation, these have minimal impact if the environment in which people work and the processes and resources used to get their job done continue to drive them nuts.

As in our earlier sporting analogy, you can't expect the team to win if they don't have what they need to honour the code and play their best game.

For sustainable change, we need to adopt a holistic and integrated approach.

Organisations are like three-legged chairs representing people, processes, and technology. To be successful, we need to appreciate the strengths and limitations of each leg. The top of the chair (the seat) represents the relationships that pull and hold the legs together to make the chair fit for purpose. Focusing on any of the components in isolation weakens the whole structure, and the chair won't function as intended.

It's easy to construct what we need from new materials, but we often can't start from scratch or don't have the luxury of focusing all our energy and resources on what we want to build or improve. Professionally and personally, there's always plenty to be maintained and balanced.

In 2020, The Oxford Review produced a report[13] after scanning more than 3,000 studies. They found that simultaneously leading, managing, and balancing existing organisational products and services while developing and experimenting with new ones is almost impossible when using the same teams and functions that maintain business as usual. The main reason is that they require vastly different thinking, assumptions, behaviours, emotional responses, beliefs, resources, structures and systems.

Despite this awareness, it's what most organisations try to do, particularly when concurrently streamlining existing practices, enhancing, or developing additional service offers, improving performance, and reducing costs.

Many private organisations, start-ups and companies do this for commercial viability and return, but Government agency reforms and transformation programs also need to do so.

It could be argued that the challenge for Government is even greater. Each agency and portfolio operate under incredibly complex and multi-dimensional pressures, with competing and limited resources to meet current and future community expectations and needs.

Government agencies also have tighter budgetary constraints and are bound by more significant accountabilities to their nation's citizens as a larger collective. It's a massive challenge to invest in people within these agencies by providing professional development opportunities and access to the right resources to deliver sustainably while reducing costs and being innovative.

EXPERIENCE MATTERS

Jaquie Scammell is a well-respected expert on customer service culture. In her book, *Service Mindset,* she explains that the way employees feel about the organisation they work in contributes to the service they provide to customers.[14]

Employee experience feeds customer experience, and what I respect most about Jaquie's work is her human-centred approach to enabling teams to develop and deliver quality services.

We attach meaning to what happens at work and home, and thoughts and feelings about our interactions impact our experience and how we work individually and collectively.

> People's experience matters, and if employees aren't heard, understood, and enabled to deliver what they're there for, everyone suffers.

It sounds fabulous when organisational goals relate to delivering value. But if people don't feel supported with what they consider to be the basics, additional or expanded outcomes probably won't be delivered.

People's experience matters, and if employees aren't heard, understood, and enabled to deliver what they're there for, everyone suffers.

CULTURE SHOCK

The first time I was hard hit by people feeling unsupported by their organisation was more than 12 years ago as an internal Human Resources advisor. It was my first week as an irritatingly over-optimistic and super-keen outsider, responsible for presenting the results of the company's most recent culture survey to the senior clinical managers of a hospital.

Although there were a few pockets of high performing teams, the organisation also had its fair share of problems. Some team results were horrid: staff reported an embedded culture of bullying, harassment, and underperformance, and little had changed since a survey two years earlier.

To be blunt, it didn't say much for the support people received from Executives or HR because, in many areas, the culture had deteriorated even further. Having never delivered culture survey results in other roles, I was a complete rookie. But being ex-military, I considered myself reasonably hardened to whatever came my way.

My 'nothing alarms me', 'I've got this', evidence-based approach to delivering the results was unempathetic, arrogant, and incredibly naïve.

As the sole HR representative in the room telling people how bad their culture was, I copped the full force of people's anger. The reaction was not surprising given I presented to the very managers deemed responsible for the poor culture. I was telling them more of what they already knew and dealt with daily. I also represented the corporate teams they felt were letting them down.

Emotions were incredibly high, and I wanted to crawl into a cave and never come out. Worse still were reports from the managers that previous results were used as a big stick to belittle them and beat them even harder. Executives and the HR team that I was part of were slammed for not caring, not understanding, and not giving them the support needed to fix the problems they struggled with – all of this on top of the high-pressure, 24/7 clinical challenges of a hospital.

I felt like the sacrificial lamb and the ogre that day, with no real preparation for the reaction to come. If my colleagues had warned me, I was certainly too proud to hear it.

During the presentation, I was in so much shock that I froze, did my best to listen to whatever came at me during the one-hour ordeal, and calmly waited for people to lower their pitchforks.

Using the same words that I hate hearing from other consultants, I had told them the time with their own watches. The first impression I'd made was a far cry from what I felt or how I wanted to be of service.

> Trust is a decision quickly followed by behaviour; you can't fake it, and you need to be human to receive it.

Trust is a decision quickly followed by behaviour; you can't fake it, and you need to be human to receive it.

Beaten and bruised

My delivery of those results was embarrassingly off the mark. Given the earlier survey history, it was no surprise when one of the managers pulled me aside afterwards to say, 'Well, you got your tits ripped off'.

It was a moment of extreme humility, but I must have appeared humble and willing to learn because her comment was quickly followed by an offer of coffee and a chat that I gratefully accepted.

Trust is also instinctual, based heavily on emotional signals regarding whether we should partner with someone, openly and honestly.

Although I wondered why no one stuck up for me during the presentation, the manager's acknowledgement of what happened and her care and kindness was invaluable. With her reputation, support, and access to people with aligned goals, I understood the issues in more detail, built a significant network of my own, slowly developed the credibility needed to serve people best, and restored faith in myself and with others.

The willingness and commitment to learn and stretch ourselves is essential to overcome challenges and achieve better outcomes.

> The willingness and commitment to learn and stretch ourselves is essential to overcome challenges and achieve better outcomes.

To shift from being an outsider to offering valuable service, I had to listen to the wisdom of elders and those doing it tough. I put what I learnt into practice, and together we did the hard yards to advocate for, support and achieve enterprise-wide change.

I let go of posturing myself, the Executive or HR, and by adopting a more humble, open, and partnered approach, I learnt how to serve better and belong.

Our need to belong

Fiona Robertson's book, *Rules of Belonging*, highlights that organisational culture is driven behaviourally and subconsciously by our need to belong.[15] Our family recently moved interstate. While this meant significantly more remote working with my existing clients, my husband and children had to build connections and friendships at work and school from scratch.

During his first month at a new school, I watched and listened to my son Hayden. He had to check out what the other kids do, figure out what is cool and uncool, determine what works in making new friends, and build individual relationships from scratch until accepted by a circle of peers. After a range of success and failure and a few days of feeling lost, he quickly figured out the rules of belonging for the kids he wanted to be friends with. It's nice to see that his experiments are working. As his mother, I do my best to respect and trust that Hayden can and will figure out which groups will be the healthiest for him.

Just as Hayden paid attention to the rules that allowed him to fit in and choose which behaviours and friends to adopt, the same goes for us when we start new jobs, change organisations, or move teams. It's one thing to consider what works for us and another to understand what will be beneficial more broadly.

Fiona Robertson offers wise words of warning in that the rules of belonging may not always serve the organisation's purpose.

In many workplace cultures I've worked with, there have always been pockets where the rules needed to break completely for the business to lead, adapt and deliver more holistic organisational and community needs. Siobhan McHale's book, *The Insider's Guide to Culture Change*,[16] emphasises the need to break behavioural patterns and the systems that embed them. As in all cases for change, this is easier in theory than in practise.

The social pull of the people we connect with can sometimes result in us all suffering from bias and lead to accepting what we've always done.

> The social pull of the people we connect with can sometimes result in us all suffering from bias and lead to accepting what we've always done.

Organisational change can be super challenging in a culture of silence, or yes-people, who further cement what may be limited and very siloed thinking. This occurs when we value our similarities and ability to stay as we are, more than the need to question and change the status

> Creative conflict, difficult conversations and alternative perspectives lead to innovation.

quo.[17] It's particularly so if we feel that the changes will create discomfort, sacrifice or loss.

You only need to remember the last time you embarked on a journey to get fit, eat healthier, or give up something you enjoyed that no longer served you, to appreciate the pain of killing off old habits to adopt new ones.

Creative conflict, difficult conversations and alternative perspectives lead to innovation.

You must make it safe to be different if you want to design and implement new ways of working that deliver what is aspired to in organisational visions, strategies, business plans, and service metrics.

KEEPING IT REAL

Conversations with people I respect and admire show that accepting imperfections and embracing our human nature connects us with ourselves and each other.

In writing this book, I have been inspired by the wisdom of people who appear in the most unexpected places and times.

From what I've read, researched, and experienced, empathy, honesty and reliability are generally acknowledged as anchors for trust. It's important to feel and find the meaning behind behaviours, reveal the truth, and consistently show up.

Yet, I've always felt this wasn't enough because my lived experience (and that of people I've worked with) has always been more convoluted. Some frustrating nuances seem to be missing.

I searched for an approach that captured the complexity while still being easy to remember and apply. It was a struggle to find something that offered depth and clarity when efforts to connect with others weren't entirely on the mark.

In pulling apart what could have better prevented many professional and personal fails, it became clear that the intersections, not the foundations, needed revisiting.

From the collective wisdom of many, I understood that we need to give our HEART+SOUL for trust.

The HEART + SOUL of trust

Honesty

Empathy

Accountability

Reliability

Trust in others

Sincerity

Openness

Understanding

Lasting focus

Figure 1: HEART+SOUL of Trust

Look closely at the intersections, and you can see the nuances between empathy, honesty and reliability.

From the realisation that we need all these competencies to establish and nurture relationships, I wrote a blog article on trust being a little word with plenty of strings attached.

It would be nice to cherry-pick what we're good at and roll with those, but our messages fail to connect when we focus on what works for us. That's because it's not about what we want or being in our comfort zone; it's about who we are trying to connect with.

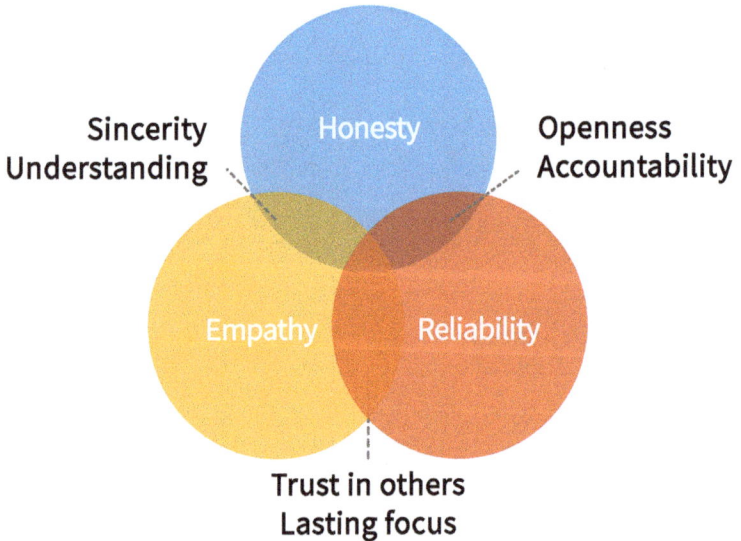

Figure 2: HEART+SOUL model

When we commit to providing these competencies for others, we create an environment for natural partnerships at all levels to support and build better work cultures. That doesn't mean you won't be disappointed from time to time, but at least you know you're giving everything you can before moving on.

In giving gracefully, we strengthen how we operate from within and grow as leaders along the way.

In giving gracefully, we strengthen how we operate from within and grow as leaders along the way.

The story of how I developed the HEART+SOUL acronym and more detail on this model is in Part Two, so feel free to jump ahead.

When leading and implementing change, the most time-consuming elements involve confusion over what is changing and why. People don't always understand or validate the meaning this has for others. This leads to an inability to acknowledge and work through the red flags of distrust that can destroy efforts to lead, influence and deliver.

THE RED FLAGS OF DISTRUST

Working in a distrusting organisation is like being recruited for an elite soccer team then being blindfolded, told to forget everything you did for selection, kept on the bench all season, blamed when the team loses, and watching more expensive players get hired to repeat the process.

No leader in their right mind would do this intentionally or let it happen on their watch, yet organisational cultures can be inherited, and unhelpful ways of working form slowly over time before becoming embedded.

These are some of the most common warning signs or red flags you need to look out for and address:

- Work submitted by individuals and teams is hidden, re-edited, pulled apart and de-scoped with little or no feedback on why it wasn't fit-for-purpose.
- Subject matter experts intentionally excluded from meetings where their insights and recommendations would be valuable because they don't agree with their immediate Manager or Executive.
- People micromanaged and told what to do, thereby stifling expertise and driving team underperformance.
- An overreliance on external industry experts to fix problems instead of connecting with employees who likely have the capability and capacity to offer and implement solutions but haven't had the opportunity.
- Significant organisational changes happen without genuine consultation and understanding of the operational impacts.
- Performance measures hold people accountable, even though they haven't been given the knowledge, resources, or support to perform.

- People don't feel safe to call out when things don't feel right.
- Little issues fester and develop into much larger, preventable problems. These are sometimes called watermelon projects, where everything is reported green to the Executive until it goes live, then when cut down the middle, people experience red.

If you recognise any of these in your organisation, it's easy to see that cultural shifts aren't just about engagement, communication, and training.

Red flag practices are reactions to larger driving forces demonstrating that now is time for a change. Drivers can occur quickly or be more evolutionary.

Think about what happens when new political parties come into power, new technologies are introduced, medical discoveries made, and societal expectations shift on what is and isn't acceptable. We're always changing the way we do things.

I was reminded of this recently when looking through childhood books telling of pipe-smoking Dad carrying his briefcase home from work, stay-at-home Mum doing the dishes in an apron, and children wearing gender-assigned clothing, playing with gender-assigned toys. Heaven forbid being a blended family, having two mums or two dads, or a boy who would rather wear dresses. There certainly wasn't any recycling either!

Just as what we wanted and needed when we were three isn't what we want or need as adults, our experience shapes our feelings, thoughts, behaviours, and needs. What might have been ok yesterday or even today might not serve us tomorrow.

When the direction, goals and aims of the organisation or business have shifted, we need to own and address the existing structures, systems, processes, and people that no longer support the required performance. The ability for businesses to rapidly adapt and evolve is vital when considering how quickly external influencers can impact what, how, when, and who in organisations deliver.

It's also worth acknowledging that people in cultures of distrust have heard, seen and felt the pain of misunderstood, unrealised, or poorly managed change, reform projects, programs, or transformation efforts before.

For people in this space, burning questions need honest answers:

- What will be done differently this time?
- Why should we believe you?
- What's in it for us to do the work to change?
- What are the consequences if things stay the same?

THE VALUE OF TRUST

Leadership is a broad, multi-faceted and very personal capability. It is the first thing to be tested and blamed when trying to shift in times of uncertainty.

Business requires leadership at all levels for individual and collective advantage; it is the capability most needed within ourselves and in the service of others.

In a 2019 study, Karen Hendrikz and Amos Engelbrecht examined leadership in ethical behaviour and decision-making. They iden-

> You can't force trust in leadership or cheat your way to success.

tified the foundational elements of transformational, servant, authentic and ethical leadership as trust, self-mastery, empowerment, and accountability.[18]

You can't force trust in leadership or cheat your way to success.

More broadly, teams and organisations' ability to perform and deliver services they're proud of rests on whether people operate in a culture that gives them the support and freedom to do so. We feel high trust cultures before we see them, but the benefits are precious and tangible.

Paul Zak shared the following statistics in a Harvard Business Review article on the benefits of trust in organisations:

> *Compared with people at low-trust companies, people at high-trust companies report 74 per cent less stress, 106 per cent more energy at work, 50 per cent higher productivity, 13 per cent fewer sick days, 76 per cent more engagement, 29 per cent more satisfaction with their lives, 40 per cent less burnout.*[19]

Best Practice Australia (BPA) are experts in organisational

culture research. Over 25 years, they surveyed more than 753,000 individuals, conducted surveys in more than 900 organisations, and worked with over 1,200 benchmarking partners.

Many years ago, I had the privilege of learning from BPA's co-founder and Director of consulting services, Jacqui Parle. She completely ramped up my understanding of the complexity of culture, taught me how to leverage the insights obtained by measuring it, and significantly grew my ability to identify strategies that best support and enable organisational success.

For more information on BPA and to access their expertise go to www.bpanz.com

Valuing the knowledge of BPA and experiences across multiple industries and work cultures, here is a comparison between distrusting and trusting organisations:

Distrusting	Trusting
People are under constant scrutiny and feel lucky to survive independent reviews, restructures, or company closure.	The organisation becomes what it aspires to be.
Deliver inconsistently, employee morale is low, and customers frequently don't get what they need.	The organisation is a pleasure to work in and delivers consistently better outcomes.

Spend more time, energy and resources putting out fires and trying to resolve issues.	Supports people and business development with structure and ways of working that enable continuous improvement.
Fail to listen and understand why things are or are not working.	Establish partnerships with service delivery teams to work through issues and co-design solutions.
Focus too heavily on mitigating risks and hiding issues.	Allow people to be human and truthful about challenges and risks before they become issues.
Prioritise own needs.	Focus on creating and developing relationships with employees and customers to understand what success means.

Table 2: Distrusting v Trusting

Trust is non-negotiable for success; it sounds obvious and straightforward, but with so much meaning and complexity attached, it's sometimes difficult to give.

I appreciate that your experiences, however similar, are different from mine – and could be better or worse. In respecting your expertise, and before we cover some of the broader challenges, let's bring it back to you.

REFLECTION

The HEART + SOUL of trust

Honesty   **S**incerity

Empathy   **O**penness

Accountability

Reliability   **U**nderstanding

Trust in others   **L**asting focus

As someone who wants to make a difference, which elements of the HEART+SOUL of trust will require more focus and effort?

What are you prepared to give and sacrifice to change?

For the people who are holding up red flags:

- What will be done differently this time?
- Why should they believe you?
- What's in it for them to partner with you?
- How will you work together?
- What support will be available for people who might struggle?

What are the consequences if things stay the same?

CHAPTER 3

CHALLENGES FOR TRUST

Without challenge, there is no growth and no sense of triumph in achieving the outcome. Life is full of challenges; success comes from the lessons we learn and the changes we make to adapt and grow further.

We often bring in advisors, consultants, and contractors to fix problems or create strategies and plans for permanent managers and employees to deliver to address internal challenges. These external efforts can compound the problem unless those providing the advice are respected as intimately understanding the business and its culture.

> Without challenge, there is no growth and no sense of triumph in achieving the outcome. Life is full of challenges; success comes from the lessons we learn and the changes we make to adapt and grow further.

TRUST

PREPARE FOR CONFLICT

Many years ago, during a job interview, I was asked if I was able to parachute in like a black-ops operative, break through glass ceilings, rappel down, and clean up the mess.

I had been in the military, and with continuing respect to those still serving, the corporate world is vastly different. It was the strangest question I'd ever been asked, but I chuckled and appreciated the interviewer's honesty about doing what needed to be done.

As I'm strangely blessed and cursed by the thrill of a challenge, and with what a mate calls a delusional level of optimism, I said 'Yes' and have responded to similar calls to action ever since.

The reason behind the black-ops analogy was apparent. Distrusting cultures are tough – mentally, emotionally, and physically. The sustained effort to combat unhelpful and often toxic feelings, thoughts, and behaviours can push people to their limits and sometimes to the point of no return. Working in these environments over long periods can also be traumatic and morally challenging.

Describing workplaces in this way might seem overly dramatic, but the damage these cultures create can run deep, lasting long after people have the courage and capability to leave. The torment people feel when not enabled or trusted to do what they are employed to do, isolated from contributing, questioned to a point where they doubt their capabilities and have work reduced without reason or explanation, could be considered

52

a form of professional gaslighting. This term describes the systemic manipulation and control that makes people question their perspective and self-worth.[20] Whether an intended outcome or not, the effects of persistent negative behaviours that undermine and exclude employees from connecting with others, and contributing to what they have been employed for, can be hard to manage and bounce back from.

When you're fresh and new to an organisation or have just joined a team that is suffering, you can sense their pain within minutes – and sometimes within seconds – of walking through the door.

Even for the most optimistic newbies or outsiders, it's terrible to have those initial impressions confirmed within your first few days or weeks. It might come in the form of remarks, such as 'Oh look at you, how cute, that shine won't last long.' 'Get some time up, and you'll see things differently.' 'You haven't been beaten by the system yet.' 'Yeah, we know it's shit, but this is what the Executive wants.' Or even 'I just turn up to get paid now'.

A 2018 study[21] by Julia DiBenigno examined the challenges faced by external consultants and experts to gain influence in the face of manager and employee scepticism and distrust. It found that they first need to overcome four key points of conflict.

Firstly, employees can feel that meetings with externals are an unhelpful distraction. This is particularly the case if the last engagement employees had with a consultant failed to produce the intended results.

Secondly, external experts often fail to deliver because, as outsiders, they lack a deeper understanding of people's issues within the organisation. It's hard to understand without adequate access or time with appropriate people on the inside. Furthermore, if you're a consultant called in to address cultural issues, people may not feel safe enough to provide context or deeper insights needed to inform and support change.

Thirdly, confusion over the power relationship between the external expert/consultant and the person engaging might be ambiguous.

Fourthly, on a personal note, permanent employees and external consultants usually do not bear similar characteristics and backgrounds, so rapport building can require extra effort.

The study focused on external people coming into an organisation, but internal executives and managers can also experience these challenges with operational teams.

EMPLOYEES AND CHANGE

Cultural change requires an all-inclusive mindset and behavioural shifts to enable multi-disciplined teams and multi-functional operations for holistic, higher-value benefits.

As a consultant, it's common to be engaged for work with a single area or a group of smaller teams, but on a larger scale, people have often been impacted by restructures, shared services transitions, outsourcing arrangements, and faux transformations. All of which contribute to what is felt across entire organisational systems.

People who love change are excited because they're connected, have control over what is happening, and trust that the result will be worth their effort. The impact of the change on who they are and how they will work has been carefully considered and worked through to benefit them.

> Cultural change requires an all-inclusive mindset and behavioural shifts to enable multi-disciplined teams and multi-functional operations for holistic, higher-value benefits.

When the people side of change hasn't received the necessary respect or attention, problems often don't surface until it's too late. That is because executives don't get the benefit of hearing casual banter among teams.

Some of the saddest examples of employee's views of change that I've heard over the years include:

- 'I want to believe this is possible, but we've heard it all before, we did the preparation – and then nothing.'
- 'Five lines in a strategy document with a new name and slightly different catchphrases won't help. What a joke.'
- 'This plan doesn't even make sense; they don't know what we do, and that won't work here.'
- 'I'm just waiting for the next piece of strategy to drop over the fence.'

- 'Just do what Exec wants, it's churn work, but they won't listen.'
- 'I feel like a flogged horse, and I'm sick of being kicked in the guts.'
- 'I'm burnt out and feel like a beaten housewife...I hate saying that, but it's how I feel.'
- 'I'll outlast you and your ideas – just as I have with every other Director and CEO.'
- 'Hopefully, we'll get a different Manager, and we can all move on.'
- 'Let's just wait until they (the consultant) get caught in the politics and can't deliver either.'
- 'I wouldn't even know what they (The Senior Leadership Team) looked like if they walked the floor.'

These statements are deep-rooted and come from a place of frustration and exhaustion after many failed attempts to turn things around.

To take the edge off shockingly low morale, people focus on what they can do elsewhere. Not surprisingly, workplace productivity suffers, as does mental health.

If you already have a healthy and thriving culture, congratulations! The reason I've painted a grim view of the challenges is that sometimes it's better to prepare for the worst and work from the ground up.

Culture change can be like a marathon, so don't expect people to run uninjured with a great time if they're on the couch, eating junk food, and don't even own a pair of runners.

It starts with being honest about where things might currently be and going in with your eyes, ears, and mind wide open.

ACKNOWLEDGING DISTRUST

The previous examples demonstrate a lack of faith in how an organisation is run and distrust in those responsible for leading and managing it.

> Culture change can be like a marathon, so don't expect people to run uninjured with a great time if they're on the couch, eating junk food, and don't even own a pair of runners.

Despite courses and self-help resources on body language, building trust and learning how to detect untruths, it's hard to determine fact from fiction when interacting with others.

Three recent studies[22, 23, 24] on lie detection identified that practised lies were almost impossible to differentiate from the truth, even when using verbal, non-verbal cues and functional magnetic resonance imaging (fMRI) scans that measure and map the brain's activity.

Even if regarded as a subject matter expert and contextual guru, we're still relying on our judgment based on previous experience and what we believe to be true and trustworthy.

> By first acknowledging when trust is absent and respecting the challenges along the way, you can open dialogue and make a decision to trust easier.

In fairness, without firm evidence, it's tough to determine whether we should put our faith in others and whether they, in turn, should trust us.

By first acknowledging when trust is absent and respecting the challenges along the way, you can open dialogue and make a decision to trust easier.

The best news is that the ability to offer and create trust can be learned and developed.

Trust is routinely called out as a key component for leading and managing organisational change to achieve long-term and sustainable benefits. In practice, greater focus is often on avoiding costs and mitigating risks to change.[25]

When championing openness and safety for people to be autonomous, adapt and continuously improve, consider that the risk-focused approaches that serve us in many ways can also be misused and become a blocker.

Trust is inherently risky – you need to be comfortable and prepared to work through what is feared.

Trust is about relationships. Even if your primary focus is technological transformation, multiple non-technical aspects need to be considered, navigated, and addressed in the first instance.

Depending on your instincts, preferences, and skills, it's reasonable and human to expect some challenges to be more complex and difficult than others. Without getting into the variable details, it's worth noting some common challenges.

SEVEN SIGNIFICANT CHALLENGES

The challenges for developing high trust organisations are incredibly complex because culture is not just about how we do things around here.

A review of multiple studies[26, 27, 28, 29, 30] on organisational culture found that culture influences and is influenced by social interactions. Acceptance and efforts to change existing business practices largely depend on the level of confidence individuals and teams have in their own experience and ability to control the change, and their relationships with immediate managers and colleagues. For change to be sustainable and scalable, we also need confidence in people who immediately report to us, whether formally or informally, and the organisation as a collective to successfully implement and embed changes.

Based on the research and the verbal face punches clients (and I) received from getting things wrong in the past, the seven significant challenges learned are:

1. Trust is contextual.
2. Emotions drive the decision.

3. Intensive focus requires discipline and energy.

4. Trusting others is risky.

5. It can be more time consuming than what you're prepared for.

6. The return isn't obvious, particularly to those not involved.

7. You are not in control of other people's decisions or actions, so there is uncertainty in the outcome.

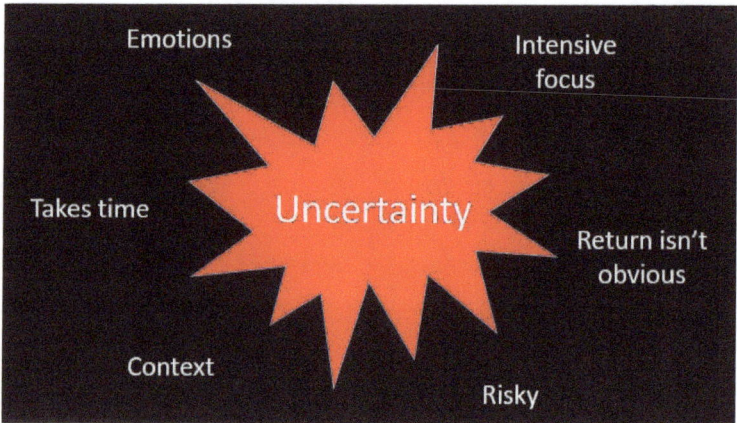

Figure 3: Challenges to trust

Accept that challenges are multi-faceted. Let go of your expectations and allow the people with whom you're trying to develop trust to guide the relationship's direction and pace.

1) Trust is contextual

Context can be a considerable challenge in environments of distrust, toxic behaviour, and micromanagement. In this context, people are not supported towards positive outcomes because they don't feel safe sharing information, experience, alternative thoughts, or solutions.

Even if you're considered skilled in shifting cultures and managing behaviours, trust in one context is not automatically transferable to others.

This was well-illustrated over coffee with a former colleague. We had each started working with new clients and were venting our frustrations at having to prove ourselves from the ground up yet again. It wasn't until we shared our 'Don't you know who we are and what we've done?' thinking that we identified our somewhat arrogant and unrealistic expectations. The CEO of one company trusted us to help with complex issues, but it did not mean we would have the same relationship with all CEOs. It was obvious in hindsight but an embarrassing realisation at the time.

> Accept that challenges are multi-faceted. Let go of your expectations and allow the people with whom you're trying to develop trust to guide the relationship's direction and pace.

It doesn't matter how good you are, or were, with an organisation, team or other people; every approach to a relationship is entirely different.

Respecting context is particularly important for anyone who works or partners with different individuals, teams, and organisations.

Just as you wouldn't give the keys to your car to someone

> It doesn't matter how good you are, or were, with an organisation, team or other people; every approach to a relationship is entirely different.

you'd just met, my friend and I had to prove ourselves repeatedly in different environments and offer more to build new relationships.

The reported needs between organisations could be identical. The top-level descriptions of challenges and issues might be similar, and even the patterns of behaviours that may be creating problems could be the same. But the context and the people in them are always unique.

Throughout this book, we'll focus on the psychological considerations, knowledge and experience of your environmental factors that need to be understood and respected. Contextual considerations include the physical spaces people occupy, political contexts, socio-economic conditions, and the cultures of the communities that surround or support you.

2) Emotions mess with rational thinking

The problem with emotions is that they happen regardless of whether or not we want them to surface.

Even if you have an extensive range of skills for managing emotions in yourself and supporting others, what we feel when it comes to change isn't always the rational or politically correct response we're hoping for.

The higher the loss or risk we experience or perceive, the more intense the emotion, and everyone responds differently. In times of stress, our reactions to events aren't always ones we're proud of.

> The problem with emotions is that they happen regardless of whether or not we want them to surface.

It's not unusual for people to experience emotional shock when they blurt out what they're feeling, and then be overcome by additional feelings of surprise and guilt over their thoughts becoming public.

Emotional responses can be embarrassing, uncomfortable, unwanted – and unpredictable – so accept that this is a natural part of any change process.

Even with trust, emotional shock can still occur, and your reaction to your own or other people's feelings can be difficult to manage – particularly if those feelings challenge your code of values and beliefs.

> Emotional responses can be embarrassing, uncomfortable, unwanted – and unpredictable – so accept that this is a natural part of any change process.

This book does not address accepting and managing emotional responses in detail. For more on this, Daniel Goleman's books on emotional intelligence provide a wealth of expertise and knowledge. In particular, *Working with Emotional Intelligence*[31] was invaluable early in my career. It was frequently referred to in the Royal Australian Air Force's Adaptive Culture Program and significantly shaped my awareness and ability to work with and manage challenging emotions across many areas of my life.

3) Intensive focus can be exhausting

Genuine trust-building requires complete attention, energy, patience, and focus for intentional empathic listening. This type of listening is all about the person telling the story, with listeners completely engaged in hearing, feeling, and understanding what is spoken and unspoken.

Intensive focus is hard work, but when people know and feel they have your undivided attention, it provides an amazing space to be open and discuss things that bother them – but which they may never have had the courage or ability to express.

This challenge is most noticeable when working with teams and facilitating groups. If people can't focus, then voices aren't heard. People become distracted by the noise around them, and the purpose of the interaction and what we need to achieve can be completely lost.

Think of a meeting where someone is like a stuck record – it's usually the result of not feeling heard. If the topic is urgent or important, they'll repeat themselves until someone meaningfully acknowledges what they're saying, offers clarity, or provides an opportunity to obtain answers for the issue in question.

Acknowledging what people are experiencing and offering your undivided attention reduces noise and provides others with the ability to focus.

The more complex the issue, the greater the concentration required to ensure you don't get caught up in the noise. You need sufficient depth in understanding to focus on how to support calm and effective shifts.

> The more complex the issue, the greater the concentration required to ensure you don't get caught up in the noise. You need sufficient depth in understanding to focus on how to support calm and effective shifts.

Remembering the earlier statement that challenges are non-linear, the emotional and mental gymnastics to work through barriers can be exhausting, so be sure to check your energy, practise good self-care, recharge, and support others to do the same.

4) Trusting others is risky

Before you tackle the mountain, you need to trust your ability and believe that the risk of the climb is worth the view.

There is a lot of perceived and real intrinsic risk in trusting someone.

When people say 'Trust me', they're missing the point. Others will decide this for themselves based on feeling comfortable

> The fastest way to earn someone's faith in you or what you're about to do is to give them your trust first.

and safe to share, not because someone tells them it's ok or that they should.

The fastest way to earn someone's faith in you or what you're about to do is to give them your trust first.

For this to work, what you say must be genuine. The receiver must know that what you're sharing and doing is personally risky for you, but you're doing so because the knowledge you're providing is personally valuable for them. There's always an element of danger in doing so, but to receive, you have to give.

If this is challenging, consider applying the HEART+SOUL competencies in reverse order. Think about the emotional and rational examples necessary to build the evidence base for your own decision-making, and confidently lead with trust by asking:

- What does it take for someone to earn your trust?
- Are your criteria reasonable in the circumstances?
- Are these criteria reasonable for the people you need the relationship with?
- Should others apply the same criteria to you?
- Could you consistently live up to the criteria?
- In not trusting others, what opportunities and relationships do you risk losing?

5) *Trust takes time to build*

In leveraging research and literature, I'm not saying anything new when I write that trust is not about us. It's about the person or people we want relationships with, and the decision on whether to trust us rests with them.

Because of this, timeframes for others to feel confident in putting their faith in us is an uncontrollable variable. Even in time-constrained situations, we still don't control their decision. Whatever expectations we have of how long it might take to build a solid relationship with someone, it's best to leave assumptions at the door.

Accepting this allows you to build relationships and behaviours for the goal, adopt more realistic thinking to accept what others are working through, and create space for them to meet you halfway.

Great relationships happen when we focus on what is necessary for a higher purpose and invest time without personal expectations.

When working with chronically distrusting individuals and teams, I openly acknowledge and empathise with what they're feeling and restate that the aim, with their help, is to make things slightly less uncomfortable.

> Great relationships happen when we focus on what is necessary for a higher purpose and invest time without personal expectations.

This approach goes a long way towards achieving ultimate longer-term goals. It opens the channels for communication, elevates them as the experts and decision-makers by asking for their help, and retains hope that trust may come further down the line.

In support of what we can control in relationships, Part Two of this book offers a model, and Part Three provides a practical way to apply it. The intent is to support your ability to adapt what I've provided to suit your greater good.

6) *The return isn't obvious*

In a world of quick wins and benefits measured by performance indicators predominantly focused on time and money, it can be hard to put a defined measure on how we work with others.

Despite culture survey and customer experience metrics relating to trust in people or an organisation's brand, the time needed to realise the benefits of trust can be more than some people are willing to give and accept.

Over the years, I've witnessed executives and teams physically and psychologically break under pressure to produce immediate results or drive enterprise and business changes without the time to adequately process or think before delivering.

These breaks are mostly the result of relentless multidimensional forces pushing for instant solutions, which can falsely diminish the importance of meaningful consultation and partnership with the people most impacted by the quality of what is implemented.

Our value as leaders is to invest time to think, question, understand, and partner in ways that simultaneously grow us and the people we need to serve and inspire.

Fight the urge to jump in before fully engaging with the people who need to deliver. That will outweigh the pain of regret from speaking or acting too soon without contribution from those who need to own the change.

The main thing to remember is that trust is a long-term goal, and if you can establish it quickly and effortlessly, you probably don't need this book. Generally, it can be more a labour of love, patience, and development over time.

> Our value as leaders is to invest time to think, question, understand, and partner in ways that simultaneously grow us and the people we need to serve and inspire.

7) Uncertainty can be hard to accept

Go with trust, and the rest you'll figure out with people as you go.

A word of caution, if you need proof to believe that positive change is a given, have difficulty in testing and adjusting toward an outcome, and can't genuinely empathise with people before working through things, a leadership role might not be for you.

If it isn't, then that's ok because leaders need followers and fighters for the cause. It is just as honourable and courageous

> Go with trust, and the rest you'll figure out with people as you go.

to recognise and call out when you're not the best person to lead. Recognise when you can offer greater value elsewhere.

Trust is not about technical mastery; it's about being human at work, allowing others to see and feel that you care more about them and how you work as a team than about the strategic plan. The outcomes are important because we're all in the business of providing services, but how you get there with the people involved will determine the level of success achieved and its sustainability long after you leave.

When it comes to making significant shifts, empathising with the disappointments people might have felt over the years, acknowledging the uncertainty they face again, and sharing your feelings is vital.

In chaotic spaces, uncertainty can be frightening and what people need is clarity, calm, and assurance. This is heightened when it involves changes to work roles and possible shifts away from the comfort of where people currently work and with whom.

Be open about what is known, what is up in the air, what could be hard work to resolve, and focus on how to make things less uncomfortable. It can make a massive difference when supporting people to own and work through things.

For solidarity in times of uncertainty, you need to be kind, remain calm, and offer clarity when others cannot.

Uncertainty can be frustrating and overwhelming. Actions also have more impact than words. If a sense of chaos is building, focus on what you can control. If you need control, commit to consistently demonstrating:

> For solidarity in times of uncertainty, you need to be kind, remain calm, and offer clarity when others cannot.

- Acceptance of what others require to feel less uncomfortable and safe

- Incredibly high competence to work with the fluctuating emotions of yourself and others

- The ability to manage your energy, the energy of others, and prevent burnout by practising self-care and supporting others to do the same

- Inclusive professionalism where the team gets full credit for the outcomes

- Trust in the value of the intangible benefits.

WORTH THE EFFORT

The beauty of genuinely acknowledging and working through challenges is that organisational changes and business shifts can be owned and actioned with minimal direction as a natural part of continuous improvement.

You can't buy trust, but the benefits are worth more than money or status.

When meaningful
relationships
exist between
employees,
providers and
customers,
confidence
that the effort
to change
will provide
genuine value
for everyone
is priceless.

With trust, you'll have unimaginable access to information, perspectives, and ideas from individuals across teams. More specifically, in partnering with others, you're much better placed to know what it takes to provide great experiences for people and deliver quality products and services.

When meaningful relationships exist between employees, providers and customers, confidence that the effort to change will provide genuine value for everyone is priceless.

A trust-based approach to build organisational unity and commitment offers:

- Safety for people to be authentic and voice how they feel
- Openness to ideas for what could make things better
- Security in people's value by identifying and accessing their strengths
- Facilitation and support of behaviours and practices for inclusion
- Shared responsibilities
- Alignment and motivation to achieve common goals

- Confidence that people are doing the best they can
- Meaningful acknowledgment of achievements

Organisations that do this achieve more because the teams and people in them leverage diversity, have lasting focus, purposefully own the work by being connected with customers, and continuously improve their ideas.

In a recent research briefing,[32] this approach was effective in fostering strategic agility in organisations.

The increasingly popular community gardens and farms are great examples of trust-based and agile organisations. In Brisbane, Australia alone, more than 30 of these now provide opportunities for locals who want to learn how to grow organic food and be a part of the local community.[33]

Goodwill and trust are assumed while acknowledging the possibility of conflict between members. Advice for those setting up community gardens focuses on diversity, inclusion and engaging everyone – even those who might be potential vandals.[34] The significant benefit is that it encourages involvement and ownership in caring for the garden and reaping the benefits. No doubt, members of the garden projects also grow friendships and care for each other.

Beyond the garden gate, relationships are encouraged with other organisations. These expand networks and develop the maturity and sustainability of the gardens and farms as a community collective.

We draw on considerable skills to create, build, and nurture

> By making the most of people's strengths, we create leaders, advocates for the greater good, and produce positive ripple effects for shared success.

trust with others across all our life experiences.

By making the most of people's strengths, we create leaders, advocates for the greater good, and produce positive ripple effects for shared success.

REFLECTION

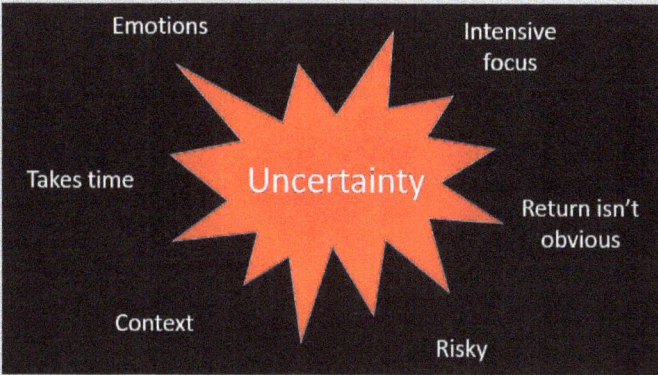

- What are the consequences of maintaining what you have now?

- What lasting outcome needs to be achieved?

- Which challenges do you need to understand better and accept?

- What are the benefits of trust in your organisation?

- How can you leverage these benefits?

- What support do you need?

- What practices are in place to manage your energy and prevent burn out?

- What support do others need?

- How will you partner with people to work through challenges as one team?

TRU

PART TWO

BE

CHAPTER 4

BUILDING THE FOUNDATION

*Building and developing trust is like
growing a strong and beautiful tree.
It takes intentional effort, nurturing,
and patience before you can sit back
and enjoy its beauty and shade.*

A 2019 Harvard Review article[35] by Jack Zenger and Joseph Folkman highlighted their study of 360-degree assessments of 87,000 leaders. They identified three foundational elements for trust. These included creating and maintaining positive relationships with other people and groups, demonstrating good judgment and expertise, and being consistent with walking the talk and exceeding people's expectations.

The study demonstrated the profoundly positive effect of being just ten per cent above average on these skills, while just below average can destroy trust. None of this is surprising, nor is the knowledge that trust ratings strongly correlate with how people rate overall leadership effectiveness.[36] Furthermore, relationships are most important because we all occasionally fail on expertise and consistency. But once a relationship is damaged (or never formed), working together can be difficult.

> People want faith in possibilities, inspiration from opportunities, the ability to add value, and clarity in how everyone will work together.

People want faith in possibilities, inspiration from opportunities, the ability to add value, and clarity in how everyone will work together.

Organisations need to develop a detailed understanding from employees of the operational challenges, focus on creating genuine partnerships with people on how to change[37] and trust leaders to lead, enable and support the teams and individuals responsible for delivery.[38]

We need to connect with people, have faith that they can do the work, and build supportive practices across the entire organisation to share knowledge, ideas, and capabilities openly.

In his book *The Code of Trust*, Robin Dreeke speaks of the complexities and nuances in creating meaningful relationships through understanding, learning, opportunity, and growth.

As a 29-year veteran of federal service in the American military, law enforcement and counterintelligence, Dreeke intimately knows the value of working with people in high-risk situations.

From his wealth of knowledge and experience, he developed the following rules to guide himself and others:

- Suspend your ego
- Be non-judgmental
- Validate others
- Honour reason
- Be generous.[39]

On the surface, it seems simple (and with practice, it can be), but after being personally and professionally burnt, trusting others and even ourselves can still be challenging. At these times, it's about digging into why the relationship matters and whether the pain of regret for not working through the challenges would be worse.

Earlier, we covered the risks of implementing quick solutions, and Dreeke's 'Suspend your ego', 'Be non-judgmental' and 'Validate others' can be particularly tough if you're a fixer who loves to roll up their sleeves and solve other people's problems.

From the perspective of a reformed fixer, this behaviour is about trying to remove discomfort when things aren't working as we think they should or would like them to.

When you remember that we're primed to avoid pain, it's not surprising that it can take a crazy amount of energy to stop us from diving in to fix things straight away. But this becomes about us and generally doesn't work in the long run.

It's far more helpful as a leader to accept that jumping to solution mode – even with good intentions – steals the opportunity from others to learn, adapt, and own the outcomes.

A simple metaphor relates to getting dressed or tying our shoes. I'm forever grateful for my parents' belief in my childhood ability to get myself sorted before going to school – albeit with some guidance.

Knowing how tested I've been over the years with my children, I'm sure it took every ounce of my parents' patience not to save their sanity and speed up the process by doing things for me.

Thanks, Mum and Dad, for allowing me to fail, learn and develop the skills I have today.

Of course, that doesn't mean we should step away entirely or not help.

> Trust is all about giving the gift of support, freedom, and flexibility. It's about demonstrating care, appreciating the value you see in people and fully believing in what is possible.

Trust is all about giving the gift of support, freedom, and flexibility. It's about demonstrating care, appreciating the value you see in people and fully believing in what is possible.

Zoë Routh, leadership expert and award-winning author, beautifully describes how to have faith in others in her book *Composure* when she describes the need to hold the other person as powerful and guide with questions.[40] Multiple research studies support the importance of this approach in facilitating and creating strong working alliances for individual, team and organisational success.[41]

As in community gardens, working alliances operate as partnerships with mutual agreement, a concentrated effort toward a common goal, and trust in each other's ability to deliver.

When we trust, we facilitate multi-disciplinary thinking, being, and belonging aligned to a bigger purpose that enables the delivery of services people value and are proud of. This also offers opportunities for individuals and teams to leave positive legacies.

IT'S NOT 'YOU'; IT'S 'WE'

The key is knowing what we can control while being connected and balanced in the hope that others might choose to walk or run beside us.

> The key is knowing what we can control while being connected and balanced in the hope that others might choose to walk or run beside us.

Responsibility for an organisation or business's health or performance never rests on the shoulders of one person or team. Every leader, manager, employee, contractor, and consultant has a part to play. We're all responsible for what we bring to the game and how we decide to play.

If you're feeling lonely, you don't need to. People within reach will likely welcome a closer partnership to improve the way work gets done.

Working-level employees have corporate knowledge and experience ready and waiting to contribute. Often, people in operations are left to sit on the bench while senior executive or external consultants develop the strategy for delivery areas to implement and sustain afterwards.

Direct line managers can be supportive, but despite best efforts to get their team a seat at the table, they might receive direct or indirect responses from senior executive along the lines of 'Thanks, but we've hired X to do that'. Employees who no longer feel trusted to do the work stop volunteering.

> Strong, high performing organisations support employees with purpose, commitment, consistent care, and a lasting focus.

In short, low trust creates low motivation, low performance, and sub-optimal results.

Even without considering the deeper psychological impacts, it's a waste of time, money, and energy when those responsible for delivery are not meaningfully involved in co-designing and presenting solutions for the organisational challenges they were recruited and retained to solve.

Strong, high performing organisations support employees with purpose, commitment, consistent care, and a lasting focus.

BEING HUMAN

Thankfully, a few years passed after the incident that a manager described as having my 'tits ripped off'. I learned lessons from those far wiser than me, and it was time to lean in and grow further.

I'd paid my dues across the operational areas by providing hundreds of workshops, mediating multiple conflicts in and among toxic teams, being a shoulder to lean on, sharing people's losses, and celebrating wins.

As an outsider, I worked hard to earn and develop the trust of managers and staff who were doing it tough and was proud to have finally built some street cred. The time came when I felt the pull to step out of consulting and practise what I preached at a more complex level from inside the operations.

Ward Services needed embedded and dedicated executive support. I respected that the management and delivery teams required significantly more support than my colleagues or I could provide with HR advisory, leadership development, and team-building activities. More importantly, I genuinely empathised with their challenges and cared about the people I'd met, despite several of them (including one who is now a close friend) doing their best to push me back to the corporate suits in the ivory tower where they candidly said I came from.

Ward Services employees are often the unsung heroes of hospitals, touching every element of the patient experience. Without them, clinical support and patient flow in and out of hospitals would come to a standstill. Collectively, Ward Services had a long-standing misrepresentation for being problem children. They were heavily siloed, frequently considered at the last minute or not at all. Their culture was consistently reported as the worst and most resistant to organisational change. They were missing dedicated executive leadership, and if any group needed love, it was this one. With three multidisciplinary divisions of around 300 people, they needed someone who could listen, understand, and provide focused representation for them at the senior level.

Eager to prove myself, I stepped up to be responsible for the large and complex tribes of Ward Services. I knew what I was in for because I'd taken the time to get to know them. I understood who they were and why they cared enough to keep fighting.

Some of my most challenging team workshops had been with this group, and they never held back on telling the HR chick exactly how it was. And with conflicting feelings of pain and delight, this continued throughout my tenure.

> Leadership is an honour given to people who generously give to grow others, traverse challenges, and celebrate success as a partnership.

Through sheer grit, I held my own, respectfully put a few cynics in their place, and the teams were shocked when I returned from maternity leave and a brief stint elsewhere to be the person some of them referred to as the Big Boss. For some, this title may be a sign of respect, but I was never comfortable with it because, at heart, I believe the only person we ever truly control and manage is ourselves.

Nuances aside, I agree that executives ultimately need to be accountable for what is delivered, but I'm a firm believer that managing or leading isn't about positioning or ownership – it's about service.

> Servant leaders are inspiring, firm, fair and believe that their mission is to serve the organisation and advocate for people delivering and receiving services.

Leadership is an honour given to people who generously give to grow others, traverse challenges, and celebrate success as a partnership.

Of all the people I've worked with over the last 20 years, few were entirely trusted or admired by their teams. To be clear, leaders are people others choose to follow without being expected, asked, or told to do so.

Ward Services had many rough diamonds who operated with grace, calm and poise. They practised servant leadership, delivering services for patients and their families, clinicians and each other under some of the most stressful, high pressure and brutal circumstances.

Servant leaders are inspiring, firm, fair and believe that their mission is to serve the organisation and advocate for people delivering and receiving services.

TRUST

Although I was in an executive role, my approach to leading Ward Services was one of service. Despite good intentions, I'm the first to admit that I didn't always get it right and that the complexity, volume, and my dogged commitment to unrealistically try and fix everything ultimately got the better of me.

Over 18 months, I got utterly schooled by informal and long-standing leaders across the services. With some regret, through not maintaining a realistic perspective of what I could and couldn't change, not taking care of my health or my family's needs, I burnt out, and, feeling like a failure at the time, I chose to leave.

But this is no sob story; the teams knew I cared. I did things differently – we worked through some major challenges to get the best possible outcomes under intense circumstances.

Whenever I could, I acknowledged and respected the value of their expertise, promoted their professionalism, and positioned them as equal partners for solutions to organisational risks and issues. It was a gift to lead a large, multi-disciplinary and genuinely agile team. Their honesty, empathy, accountability, reliability, and lasting focus educated me more than my Psychology degree and any military or professional development course ever did.

The employees in my care taught me about organisational tribes, the importance of servant leadership, accepting my humanity, prioritising my health, the immense value of believing in others when working through simple, complex, and systemic challenges, and the significance of interpersonal and interconnecting relationships.

In summary, Ward Services taught me the power of emotions at work, the importance of mastering them, and the value of high performing multi-disciplinary teams.

MASTERING BUSINESS WITH EMOTIONAL CAPITAL

'Your primary role as a leader is to create emotional wealth for competitive advantage... The ability to recognise and respond thoughtfully and creatively to your emotional experience is the most critical factor determining your success.'

– Dr Martyn Newman

As you've probably realised, I've experienced and witnessed a great deal of pain in teams and organisations over the years, and I'm calling out that managing emotions is not soft skills – it's bloody hard work!

There are plenty of helpful books and courses on emotional intelligence (EQ). I've used what worked, shared them with others, and offered guidance for people wanting or needing it. I'll never consider myself an expert, though, because we're all unique. With our experiences, feelings, and thoughts to make decisions, we behave in ways we believe are best for us at any given moment. The only person who truly knows your inner workings and what you need is you.

Martyn Newman (PhD) is a well-respected international expert in emotional intelligence and leadership. In his book, *Emotional Capitalists,* he describes extraordinary leaders as people who build successful businesses by valuing and leveraging external, internal, and intra-personal emotional capital elements.[42]

External capital relates to what customers feel and perceive about the business. Internal capital focuses on the emotional commitments held in the hearts of the people within your organisation, as seen in the energy and enthusiasm they bring to work. Intra-personal capital is the positive energy you invest and your ability to mobilise, focus, and renew others' collective energy.

When it comes to mastering a business, Nic Marchesi and Lucas Patchett founded *Orange Sky* in 2014. They fitted the back of a van, affectionately known as 'Sudsy', with a couple of washing machines and dryers, to provide the world's first free mobile laundry service for people experiencing homelessness.[43]

What started as an idea between two mates to restore dignity to people doing it tough, *Orange Sky Australia* now runs services across Australia and New Zealand. The organisation prides itself on being purpose-driven to positively connect people by working with the community to provide clean laundry, warm showers, and genuine conversation with friends. You only need to check out their website at www.orangesky.org.au to see that this is an organisation that lives and breathes emotional capital.

It's easy to focus too heavily on delivering to time and budget in the corporate world and not enough on relationships, purpose and meaning.

To develop relationships, we need to know what elements to grow within ourselves first. These involve the ability to:

- Demonstrate unconditional positive regard for people to understand them
- Have patience for where others are
- Sit comfortably in uncomfortable situations
- Silence the voices in our head so we can fully engage and connect
- Put our ego and desire to control and fix on hold
- Prioritise and practise self-care, and support others in doing this too.

The awesome thing about these qualities is that they all involve emotional intelligence, and so they are completely coachable competences – regardless of age, sex, background, profession, or stature.

All the skills that build and nurture trust are free and inclusively available when we commit to learning and applying them.

Emotional capital is a combination of learned skills that, with practise, can be developed beyond what we may think possible.

> All the skills that build and nurture trust are free and inclusively available when we commit to learning and applying them.

Most importantly, these skills are the foundation for meaningful and trusting relationships. In the workplace, this means the freedom to get stuff done faster with little resistance or interference.

Everything in this book can be a big ask, and tackling everything all at once is a recipe for overwhelm. Accepting that honesty is a non-negotiable, a quick assessment of where you're at within your current context will offer a useful baseline to determine where to direct your energy and focus first.

ABOUT YOU

Ideally, use an evidence-based leadership assessment to research insights into your emotional intelligence. The Emotional Capital Report (ECR) Self-Assessment or 360[44] provides a robust and scientifically proven method for understanding how your skills can further your success as a leader.

Numerous other assessment tools in the market can be useful to understand and develop your style as a leader, but if you're not up for a formal or scientific assessment, there are other ways you can gain some baseline intelligence for insight and growth.

If you want honesty, your approach in asking for, hearing, and accepting feedback needs to be open. The best advice I've ever received on how to do this is to listen entirely without interrupting, and, once the feedback is given, respond using one or both of the following statements:

- *'Please tell me more?'*
- *'Thank you, I appreciate your feedback, particularly about 'X.'*

Applying the HEART+SOUL of trust here creates a considerable amount of calm. It's common to hear people say that they want us to give our heart and soul, but rarely can they articulate what this means. My interpretation of this request is:

> The HEART+SOUL of trust is about connecting with the person or people you want to serve, inspire, and lead so you can grow together.

The HEART+SOUL of trust is about connecting with the person or people you want to serve, inspire, and lead so you can grow together.

We'll get into the details of what I mean by HEART+SOUL in the next two chapters, but first, let's be clear about what trust is not.

WHAT TRUST IS NOT

Trust is not respect, engagement, or environmental. It is not about a position or jumping through checklists and processes. Most importantly, trust is not the same for everyone.

If you genuinely want to be part of the privileged space and inner circle where people feel safe to be their most authentic selves, be willing to provide all the HEART+SOUL competencies.

> Words of wisdom and advice are heard more readily when they come from people we have invited in.

As you've read in the earlier fails, these competencies can't be cherry-picked based on what you're already good at or comfortable with. And they don't work through a linear application. Doing so can result in the opposite of what you're hoping for. I've learned that:

- Trying to demonstrate good intentions, establish accountability, reliability, and credibility at a rapid pace can come off as aggressive.
- Not respecting the context or challenges people face can give the impression that you don't understand or are unempathetic for where they are now.
- A long-term and lasting focus without first addressing immediate needs can lead to a perception of having a hidden agenda or pushing too much too soon.
- Being honest without having the relationship or permission to do so means you can get voted 'off the island' and miss opportunities to provide the most value at no extra cost.
- Not taking a full HEART+SOUL approach can result in a loss for multiple parties in relationships, time, money, and productivity.
- Unless you offer the complete package of trust competencies, people may find it difficult to connect with you as a human.

Words of wisdom and advice are heard more readily when they come from people we have invited in.

KNOWING WHERE TO START

Ok, so at this point, I wouldn't blame you for feeling overwhelmed and wanting to be a robot. I admit that there are days when I've not liked being human. But life is too fascinating to wish away what we have, and it's our universally similar but individual differences and unique experiences that make us colourful and interesting.

There's nothing more demotivating than feeling we must improve everything all at once, so remember the old saying about eating an elephant one bite at a time. Before taking the first bite, a great place to begin is with a quick assessment of the elephant.

We can flip the concept of a Net Promoter Score (NPS) into a Trust Score. Organisations frequently use NPS to measure customer loyalty by asking questions such as 'Would you recommend us to a friend?'

Customers rate the company on a scale of 0 (Not at all) to 10 (Extremely likely). Scores between 0 to 6 are considered detractors, 7 to 8 are passive, and 9 to 10 as promoters.[45, 46]

With similar logic, ask the following question to obtain an overall Trust Score for you and your context.

On a scale of 0 (not at all) to 10 (completely), how much do you trust [team or organisation] to deliver [outcome]?

Assess the ratings as:

- 0 to 6 = Distrust
- 7 to 8 = Low trust
- 9 to 10 = Trust

If the score is less than positive, beware of delving too deeply into what is wrong and certainly don't justify any behaviour that has led to it.

The purpose of this exercise is to acknowledge your current experience, own it, and find out what is needed to improve. To improve the rating through an outcome-focused response, it's also useful to ask what would increase this rating.

Receiving a Trust Score and understanding how to improve it will give you an overarching view or vibe to work with. Celebrate any ratings of 9 and 10. Ask for more information on what is working well, and consider how this can be scaled up and out for greater benefit.

For ratings below 8, you'll need more personal conversations that allow for greater insight, understanding and growth.

UNDERSTANDING TRUST

Use the evaluation on the next pages to dig a little deeper for factors that could block strategic and operational success.

Complete this first as an individual exercise. You can use the ratings purely for self-reflection and development, with teams or across the larger organisation to quickly assess your organisational culture's health.

Each sliding scale lines up with the HEART+SOUL competencies for trust.

If you're courageous enough to open your perspective, check your assumptions by inviting a selection of employees, managers and perhaps a trusted colleague to complete this too.

Use the ratings to facilitate discussion on possible improvements; these can powerfully demonstrate your offer to enable and support change in partnership with those who have shared their perspectives.

This exercise can produce useful and unspoken insights to support your growth and that of your team for even greater value by helping you to:

- Reflect and start conversations about trust
- Baseline the level of trust now
- See what needs to shift
- Determine priorities for improvement
- Open opportunities to co-design how things can be better
- Invite and gain commitment to action

Owning your beliefs about trust

Step 1: Assess your current state	The statements in the boxes below are on a scale from 1 (least) to 5 (most). Choose the number closest to your beliefs about trust. Rate what you consider most important within your current context. (Leave out the value and urgency columns for now.)
Step 2: Reflect on perspective	• How does your perspective serve you and others? • How does this support people? • What shift would be most beneficial, and why? • How can you change some of your thinking and behaviour for optimal results? • How can you hold other people as powerful? • What will it take for you to stay the course when things get tough? • Who could validate and challenge your perspective?
Step 3: Consider value and urgency	Based on your reflection, rank each item in order of value (low, medium, high). Decide whether you need to concentrate on it now, next, or later and create an action plan. This is where a respected leader, coach or mentor can be useful to support development and growth.

Table 3: Owning your beliefs about trust

PART 2: BE

Item	Statement	1	2	3	4	5	Statement	Value (Low, Medium, High)	Urgency (Now, Next, Later)
1	Telling the truth isn't worth the risk						It's better to tell the truth than live a lie		
2	People need to stop complaining and get it done						Investing time to understand what people are feeling and why it is important		
3	I don't want to be part of this						I own what I'm doing, how I'm doing it, and the impact on others		
4	I have too much going on right now						I'm dependable and consistent in how I show up		
5	Other people will let me down						I value and leverage the experience, knowledge, and abilities of others		
6	Emotions get in the way of progress						It's important to show people that I care and am here to support them		
7	It needs to be done this way						It's important to explore alternative options		
8	I don't understand why things aren't getting done						Understanding issues before jumping to solution mode is vital		
9	This change won't last						Delivering sustainable, quality services and value is more important than implementation		

Table 4: Telling the truth

99

REFLECTION

- To create a working alliance, how can you hold yourself and others as inclusively powerful?

- How does your perspective serve you and others in achieving organisational goals?

- If it's an accurate reflection of how others perceive you, how does this support them to succeed?

- What shift will be most beneficial, and why?

- How can you change your thinking and behaviour to increase the likelihood of organisational, team and individual success?

- What will it take for you to stay the course when things get tough?

- Who can validate and challenge your perspective for the greater good?

CHAPTER 5

HEART

Figure 4: Have heart

HONESTY AND EMPATHY

Facts are always more powerful than opinion as they are less easy to dispute, but truth-telling without empathy can come across as judgmental and cold. While this might be obvious, it must be said. Even if something is a fact and people need to hear it, it's not about applying truth at all costs.

Emotion Recognition Ability (ERA) is vital for empathy. It is the ability to recognise and interpret other people's emotions from their body language and other non-verbal cues. This is an essential skill for adapting our behaviours to build and maintain relationships.

From multiple neuroscience studies, we know that ERA stages involve perceiving other people's emotions, matching knowledge gained from previous emotional situations, and applying meaning to the emotion.[47]

This stuff requires significant cognitive skill, and as I mentioned earlier, it's why I'm not a fan of emotional intelligence and interpersonal skills being considered soft. A meta-analysis of 106 studies conducted on ERA, general intelligence, and reasoning since 2012[48] found that despite no correlation between ERA and academic achievement, there is a strong connection between ERA and general intelligence. Furthermore, sensitive people are perceived as more intelligent than less sensitive people.

I believe that the HEART+SOUL approach for trust is not linear because honesty can be a slap in the face if not paired with the other competencies.

> By combining honesty and empathy, you're in a better mindset to respectfully reveal the truth.

By combining honesty and empathy, you're in a better mindset to respectfully reveal the truth.

Honesty is one of the most difficult approaches in distrusting environments where people are micro-managed to the point of incompetence, and the term 'thrown under the bus' is part of business-as-usual conversations. But in such cultures, honesty is a rare and valuable jewel offered only by those with the finesse and courage to deliver it well.

There are always multiple viewpoints, stories, and reasons why something happened or a situation isn't what it could be. The strange thing about perspective is that it's a solo view of the world. Sure, people may share similar ideas and even agree with you, but what they think and feel below the surface can be entirely different.

Honesty might be unpleasant, but truths that need to be heard are received better when delivered with empathy.

More than words

> *'Remember, where you stand*
> *determines what you see.'*
>
> – Dr Martyn Newman

The value of seeing below the surface became crystal clear the day Robbie alerted me about night and evening staff concerns.

Robbie was a Wardsperson with what seemed like three lifetimes of experience; he'd been around so long he'd even retired and returned to work. Although he was no angel, Robbie really cared about what he did and how the hospital ran. Very much the old man of the crew, he looked out for people, and they looked out for him.

TRUST

After a couple of weeks in my role as Director, I'd been on a few shifts and was enjoying getting to know people. My approach was different from the executives before me; I worked side-by-side on shifts – cleaning, moving patients, and learning about hospital admin. The doctors and nurses saw me as another new member of the crew, and numerous Ward Services employees enjoyed my awkwardness in doing what for them were the most basic tasks. While I walked the corridors and got a feel for what inspired them and what it was like in their uniforms, I asked lots of questions about the good, bad, and horrible aspects of their work.

I was pretty happy getting to know the teams until one morning, Robbie quietly pulled me aside. Despite his age and wisdom, he seemed anxious and uncomfortable with what he was about to say. With absolute sincerity, Robbie said he wanted to trust me and felt I was trying to do the right thing, but he and some of the guys were worried.

Like so many areas across the hospital, Ward Services were under pressure to justify their budget. As Director, I needed to understand our operating costs, determine where we could achieve efficiencies and savings, and, if required, develop a business case for additional funding.

Ward Services funding was hard to win and very easy to lose. While it was understandable that clinical areas took priority, funding for support services was often the first to suffer when it came to tightening budgets.

While working alongside the crews, I asked plenty of questions, including about shifts and penalty rates. I didn't realise that Ward Services staff suspected that I was going to cut their pay.

Feeling they were always getting screwed over, Robbie heard what the others said and decided to find out for himself. I appreciated Robbie telling me how everyone felt. From conversations, I knew that people wanted greater security and that permanent vacancies were costing us more to fill casually.

Robbie's honesty enabled me to put people at ease by letting them know their pay was not going to be cut, providing early notice that we would advertise permanent roles, and offering an opportunity to those who wanted more security.

The best part of this story is that by speaking up for the team, Robbie became a hero as he spread the word, offered assurance to others and promoted the benefit of being honest and letting me know when other things came up. The ripple effects from this one interaction were invaluable. As a larger collective, we looked out for each other and became partners for continuous improvement.

Creating safety

Facts can also involve what people are feeling and why.

Our feelings often help us with being honest because when we're not congruent with our values and what we feel is right, the difference between who we are and what we're doing becomes so uncomfortable that eventually, we'll try to rebalance things. This is known as cognitive dissonance.[49]

Feelings are powerful drivers behind thoughts, conversations, and behaviours. Tuning into what people feel and asking for their perspective first is hugely beneficial.

Reflecting on the CEO story in Chapter One reminds me that the truth can be confronting, scary, and reveal multiple vulnerabilities.

I've spoken a lot about creating partnerships with people, and for this to occur, we need to create conditions for peak performance wherever possible. A lot of this has to do with safety.

A 2020 study[50] on team effectiveness found that the power distance between people resulting from differences in hierarchical position, knowledge, experience, and social status can be automatically threatening and create tension. High levels of psychological safety overcome inherent power issues when people believe they can raise concerns and challenge the status quo without negative consequences.

Psychological safety is beginning to get traction in the leadership space and where emotional capital and the ability to facilitate and sustain trust are non-negotiable. For many of my clients, the environment and physical safety are just as important. It can be the difference between life and death for those working in military, health, mental health, and justice organisations.

The ability to create or adjust your environment as a calm and neutral space can go an exceptionally long way in opening dialogue. We often don't appreciate how important this is for our culture.

*'Cultural innovations occur in
deep relationships between land,
spirit and groups of people.'*

– Tyson Yunkaporta[51]

In thinking about land, one manager I worked with joked about the 'honesty tree' we used every time we wanted to get something into the open. The office was territorial, clinical, and closed, and it was much nicer to walk outside together and sit side-by-side under the tree to chat.

Make no mistake, the topics discussed under the tree were not easy, but it took the edge off, and in the neutral space, people felt more comfortable. The conversations were still tough, and people were held accountable, but regardless of how angry anyone was, no one ever yelled under the tree, and things were far more manageable afterwards. Birds chirping and the gentle rustle of leaves helped us be calm, open to feedback, and more reflective.

Power distance and creating safety isn't all about trees, and it is a tricky one because, as my husband, Anthony, says, 'You're not the pilot of their plane'. All you can really control is you.

You can, of course, try a few things in any environment:

1. *Ask for their perspective first*

This will help identify baseline awareness and support them with taking in what is needed. It will also demonstrate your belief that they can reflect and adapt.

2. *Tap into feelings*

If you're picking up the vibe that something isn't right, chances are it isn't. Calling that out first can invite others in and create the opportunity to share what is bothering them.

3. *Manage your approach and response*

Be mindful of your own physical and emotional state. The questions you ask might not provide the answers you expect or want to hear.

If you're quick to react, people will shut down. If you're calm, you'll learn more and create space for consideration and options.

4. *Be measured and mindful of pace*

Consider what people need to know or what is useful versus sharing everything to the point of damage and overwhelm.

What is simple for you could be complicated for others. This becomes apparent if they've been dealing with an issue for three months and you've only just been made aware of it.

You could be much further ahead or behind in understanding and might need time to process the question or information.

5. *Remember that experience matters, and guide with questions*

If it's someone from an operational area and you're in

a senior position, they're likely to have greater subject matter expertise to resolve the issue.

Questions that guide people's thinking enable their power and validate the belief that they can work through what is being shared.[52]

If people start sharing, ask questions such as, 'I'd like help to understand this further, can you please tell me more about what is going on?' 'Why is it done like that?' 'What is the impact if it isn't?' and 'What needs to be done?'

6. *Validate, offer support, and seek updates*

Reflect what you've heard and the resolution they've suggested to check you've got the right message. Ask what support they need from you, and lock in an update on progress to demonstrate that you care and are available.

ACCOUNTABILITY AND RELIABILITY

Being accountable gives us control, but accountability for all things at all costs can have a counterproductive effect on performance.

Sometimes we try so hard to make things right that we forget the team or organisation's success isn't all on us. As shared earlier, I've taken on more than my fair workload in the past and have witnessed countless others unnecessarily do the same.

It's far more useful to get real and focus on the basics first.

I often use sporting analogies to remember that we are responsible for how we show up, train, play the game, and work with others. The whole team is responsible for winning or losing the game.

As the coach for my son's soccer team, I hated seeing how down the kids got when they were the goalie and missed saving a goal. Each time this happened, I got the goalie to look up, count the rest of the players on the team, and remember that the ball had to pass through everyone else on the field before it got to them. It was never just their fault for the team winning or losing; it was about everyone working together.

> Work is a team sport; organisational culture and success never rest on the shoulders of one person or a select few. Everyone is responsible.

Work is a team sport; organisational culture and success never rest on the shoulders of one person or a select few. Everyone is responsible.

If you run around worrying about what others are or aren't doing, or you're constantly filling gaps where others need to step up, at some point, your own performance will slip, and so will your health.

For the sake of your wellbeing, have realistic expectations of what you can and can't do – physically, mentally, and emotionally.

When it comes to reliability, we determine how we show up, and how often we give our best to deliver consistently and with quality. The magic is that by demonstrating the behaviours necessary for team success, you raise the bar for people to meet you.

Accepting that some days will be better than others, we're responsible for being there when others are struggling and graciously acknowledging our limitations by reaching out when we also need extra support. This is even more important if you're in a leadership role because people need to see that you're human, authentic, and real.

Remembering that whether we're in the workplace or at home, we all want to add value and offer something that has meaning and purpose.

The greatest benefits of being open about what you can't do are easing (often self-imposed and unrealistic) pressures and creating opportunities for others who want to help and be part of something more.

Ironically, calling out where you need support may encourage others to do the same, resulting in a more realistic assessment of what can and can't be achieved with existing resources and constraints. It may also enable clearer tasking and prioritisation for everyone to be better accountable and more reliable across the organisation.

TRUST IN OTHERS AND SELF

It might seem odd to have trust as a competency of trust, but this is our reminder to give if we want to receive, particularly where other people are involved, and multiple disciplines of expertise are needed to achieve the outcome.

Earlier, we acknowledged that trust is a risky business, and while it's useful to be mindful of this, the flip side is that focusing too heavily on the impact of the risk may have us perceived as overly fearful and defensive.

Risks aside, if (like the former me) you tend to be stubborn and prefer to handle things yourself, this can inadvertently push people away. In taking on too much responsibility, not only do you remove others' ability to share their experience and grow, but you miss out on things too. For example, taking on everything at work may leave you little energy to engage with hobbies or moments with family and friends. Focusing on work with little rest and no play can see you on the fast track to a personal meltdown.

I learned this the hard way. It took a life-changing emotional, mental and physical burnout, a trip to the Emergency Department to get assessed for symptoms associated with a heart attack, and an excruciatingly tough conversation with my then nine-year-old daughter Hayley telling me that I loved work more than her, to realise I had to approach things differently.

Being human and allowing others to see us for who we are under the roles, responsibilities, and professional masks works in our favour when connecting with people. I can thank my closest friends and family for that little nugget of wisdom and for keeping me sane.

I like to think that trusting others is an opportunity to grow my humility and create space for others to be involved. Shared experiences deepen relationships, and there's something in the old saying that 'it's better to give than receive', as people generally like to help where they can and feel useful.

Delegation is a great way to demonstrate confidence in someone else's ability, and it's where many of us fail. Regardless of the rationale behind not delegating, there are many reasons why putting our faith in others can be in everyone's best interests.

Delegate where you can so everyone has some responsibility for the outcome. This allows others in the team to own their space too. Everyone is employed for a reason, and giving people work they can genuinely own demonstrates a belief in their ability to deliver and offers an opportunity to shine.

> Delegate where you can so everyone has some responsibility for the outcome.

When it comes to workplace change, people often talk about 'bringing people on the journey'. But if you've heard this often enough, you don't want to be dragged along; you want to be driving, or at least have some say in where you'll end up and how you'll get there.

Trusting others means being able to delegate, enabling people to do what they've been employed to do by sometimes getting out of their way, and allowing them to offer additional value, so they stay interested.

> Faith in ourselves and others is powerful.

Faith in ourselves and others is powerful.

There's no need to profess your faith from the rooftops. The people I most respect and am drawn to are those who possess quiet confidence and belief in themselves. They have a distinct calmness because they're comfortable in who they are and what they stand for and have nothing to prove.

There is no arrogance in how they present themselves because they genuinely want to hear and understand the answers to their questions. It's reverse positioning, where they make you feel like the centre of the universe because they trust that whatever you come up with will be good.

This type of executive or high-level trust can feel weird, and if you're not completely sure you're on the mark, it can also be scary. Executive-level doesn't necessarily mean a position of formal authority; instead, it's faith of a higher order that can come from anyone who believes you're capable of more than what you expect of yourself.

This can be a heavy weight when the stakes are high, you haven't done something before, and you are in uncharted waters. There may be a real fear of letting someone down. We're the sum of our experiences; we've all failed in something and will continue to do so.

Failure is a lesson, and as much as it grates to hear that, I begrudgingly agree. The harsh reality is that failures carry varying degrees of pain, and it can take time to get the lesson, dust ourselves off, and rebuild confidence to go again. It can be tough to get up, and some people bounce back quicker or slower than others.

> To be strong, we need to trust and lead ourselves first.

To be strong, we need to trust and lead ourselves first.

As humans, we occasionally find ourselves ready with the other HEART+SOUL competencies but still find it hard to trust ourselves or others. When this happens, acknowledge it as a natural response to levelling up for a challenge you're yet to master.

We're not always going to feel 100 per cent confident in everything we do, but I'm guessing that even if there are times you don't feel it, you at least know what it looks like. If not in yourself, then certainly in others.

To commit with HEART+SOUL, we need to look in the mirror and check that we're living our truth too.

REFLECTION

- How often are you honest with yourself?
- How can you create safety for people to approach you with their concerns?
- Who does the truth serve?
- What are the consequences if the truth is not known?
- How will being honest benefit people?
- Think of a time when you received feedback in a way that matched your values and aspirations. How can you offer that same experience?
- How can you demonstrate your trust in others to deliver?
- What does 'quietly confident' mean for you? How can you model this?

CHAPTER 6

SOUL

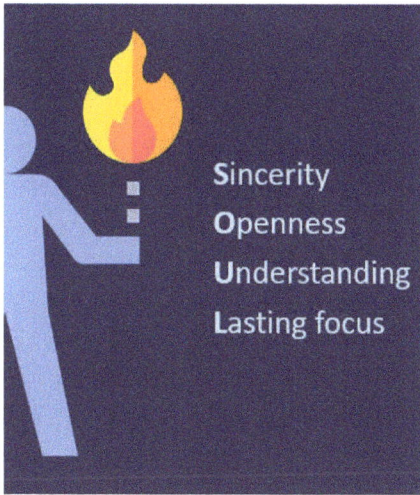

Figure 5: Build soul

SINCERITY

'Sincerity is the face of the soul...'

– Joseph Sanial Dubay[53]

We want to know that someone has our best interests at heart before we're willing to put our faith in them.

It's also fair to say that we won't get along with everyone, and sometimes people simply grind our gears. We've all been there at some point and aren't immune to it happening in future.

I've witnessed complete breakdowns of personal and professional relationships and have supported resetting people's expectations during conflict mediation and counselling through misconduct proceedings. It's a horrible feeling for everyone involved. The impacts can be far-reaching, long term, and there are no winners regardless of which side people are on.

Conflict occurs for many reasons, but what is common to all mediations and investigations are people's feelings of being disrespected and not valued.

An underlying component of the friction and resentment that follows is the real or perceived lack of sincerity. People see the other party as fake or having an ulterior motive behind what they say or do.

I believe most people want to come to work, do a great job, go home, and live happily, knowing they've contributed to society in some way. Even if you're a loner, you want to feel you've lived to your own code and are respected for doing so. What we don't want is to be inadvertently embroiled in a messy 'he said, she said, they said', physical, psychological, or emotional war at work – or anywhere for that matter. Arguments and fights occur when we misinterpret intentions, make assumptions, don't seek to understand, judge what we believe should or should not happen, and blur the lines of what is – and is not – acceptable behaviour.

I'm not trying to provide a conflict mediation lesson here, just an appreciation that when you speak with the parties involved, understand their values, and hear who they want to be in the world, you can see that behaviours, not people, are the issue. Pain is palpable, experienced by both sides, and you may never get an expected apology or closure for what has happened.

Early and sincere discussion can avoid mediation, underperformance and misconduct, but sometimes your best efforts to make peace and rebuild trust will not be enough.

You can't fake it 'til you make it with trust, so if the work to rebuild any personal friendship will damage you further, reset your expectations of the relationship, and commit to remaining professional. While still being effective, the path of least resistance is to:

- Ask questions to support acceptance of what is
- Develop strategies to move forward regardless of others' ability to meet you halfway
- Be truthful with people so they can control what they can to be slightly less uncomfortable
- Support self-management for individuals and teams to simultaneously honour the values of the organisation and their own code.

Prevention is far better than cure, and the ability to have difficult conversations requires sincerity for the message to be received as intended.

Sincerity involves genuine care in how the truth needs to be

> Sincerity involves genuine care in how the truth needs to be revealed. For the benefit of others, we need to be kind, serious, and truthful.

revealed. For the benefit of others, we need to be kind, serious, and truthful.[54]

Being **kind** is key to being sincere, and it's often an underrated quality in leadership and people management. It's easy to mention the more common call-outs for authenticity and honesty, but it's rare to read of kindness at work. We know when kindness is absent, though, because, without it, the truth can be cold, hurtful and fail to serve its higher purpose.

Sincere comes from the word **serious**. It is where depth comes into play, particularly if an apology or acknowledgment of someone else's struggle or pain is needed.

There is something about the word **truthful** that lends itself more to a presentation of facts vs feelings, and when combined with kindness, it's a nice way to consider both emotional and rational needs.

However, when there is a need to be both serious and truthful, it's not uncommon to avoid the conversation or swing between being so subtle that the message fails to hit the mark or brutal and lacking compassion in a rush to end the conversation.

At either end of the spectrum, the receiver can miss the message entirely or be so focused on the content that they don't get the broader context or intent. It's no wonder we all get into trouble sometimes.

Acclaimed sociologist, Arlie Russell Hochschild, coined the term **emotional labour** from her studies of front-line workers. As a formal or informal requirement of their employment, they need to suppress or amplify the expression of their emotions at work with customers, colleagues, and managers.[55] Some examples of high emotional labour roles include flight attendants, bill collectors, crisis support workers, police and corrections officers, military members, customer service employees, nurses, and doctors.

There are two forms of emotional labour; surface acting, where the outward expression is changed, or deep acting, where the expression is changed, and emotion suppressed to align with outward appearance.[56]

Not surprisingly, the greater the estrangement between emotions felt and displayed, the more effort required to manage it.

In an age of increasing political correctness, conflict avoidance, and the need to be more accepting of shifting societal norms, emotional labour in the workplace can be needed in general terms when things don't go to plan, and professional relationships become challenging. We are all susceptible to letting our professionalism or personal code of ethics slip.

Multiple studies have shown that the greater the gap between what is genuinely felt, what is displayed, and the length of time needed to sustain the effort, the more damaging it is for people's wellbeing.[57]

As communicators, we often assume the receiver's response will mirror our own, but this is not always the case.[58] Furthermore, the long-term benefit of the conversation often far outweighs the short-term discomfort of the moment itself.[59]

The unavoidable importance of sincerity and the impact of emotional labour became realised when I managed Brooke. From my perspective, Brooke had a brain the size of the universe, and I respected her ability to think broadly and deeply at the same time. Brooke naturally projected a quiet understanding and presence where it was easy to feel she knew far more than she let on. I respected what I considered an intellect far beyond my capacity.

Unfortunately for Brooke, I'd come from outside the organisation to win a permanent role in which she'd been acting and had been encouraged to apply for. Before I came along, Brooke believed she was doing ok. It was one thing to accept me as her manager, but an even bigger hit came a couple of months later when we needed to discuss her performance.

Brooke faced an unfair range of challenges. She was working through some significant and unstable mental health issues and was heavily medicated. As a result, things felt hazy most of the time, and she struggled to stay awake in meetings. Brooke was in a role that could be very confronting. To perform, she needed to facilitate workshops, provide support to managers for challenging people issues and deal with complicated team dynamics in cultures marred by bullying and harassing behaviours.

Brooke knew she wasn't in the right headspace, and I could see that she was struggling. She refused offers to modify her role or hours until her situation stabilised. Despite all the training and coaching provided, she just wasn't fit for the role. Brooke was, and no doubt still is, an amazing person who really cares about her performance. At the time, she was incredibly hard on herself, fiercely determined to improve, and it was horrible to hear her self-talk and what people were saying about her. To her credit, Brooke was a fighter and saw the challenges as something to overcome, but her refusal to accept that the role just wasn't for her, at least not back then, was doing her and the team more harm than good.

I'd been told that Brooke had been saved from another area that didn't work out and that if my department couldn't help her, then no-one could. With Brooke as my direct report, I felt the weight of that responsibility.

It was time to muscle up and have the conversation. Disappointingly, it doesn't matter how trained or expert others consider you; difficult conversations are exactly that – difficult.

> In difficult situations, be honest and compassionate, ensure your intentions are clear, respect multiple truths, and provide support to accept and adapt to the information.

TRUST

In difficult situations, be honest and compassionate, ensure your intentions are clear, respect multiple truths, and provide support to accept and adapt to the information.

For the conversation with Brooke, I needed to be kind, serious and truthful about her mental health and her inability to continue in the current role. I also needed to find out what she wanted to achieve and offer whatever support I could.

I'd been briefed on Brooke's past behaviours, so feeling her anxiety match my own, we went and sat in a park filled with trees. It was a beautiful day that didn't fit my feelings about what needed to be said, heard, and understood.

I started by asking Brooke for her perspective on who she wanted to be as a professional and how she was doing. I used every competency and piece of reflection in this book with outward calm, but inside my heart was racing, my mind was working overtime, and I was terrified about making the situation worse. But it wasn't about me – Brooke deserved the truth. Her statement 'I want to be treated as normal' allowed me to offer what she wanted.

After what seemed like a forever pause, I shared what I respected about Brooke and what I saw as her strengths. I said that to honour her right and need to be treated normally, I would be honest about her performance and ways to work together to support her professional goals.

The conversation went as best it could with some hardcore fluctuating emotions ranging from embarrassment, shame, helplessness, then finally anger, and outrage.

With surprising relief, the anger wasn't at me; it was for previous supervisors and managers who'd never dared to be real with her. She didn't want their pity or to be treated differently. After seeing me in the role, Brooke realised she hadn't performed it well when backfilling it before my arrival. She now understood more about what was needed, knew she wasn't hitting the mark and recognised that things wouldn't improve without personal stability and significant professional development.

Brooke was furious that the people she'd trusted hadn't been honest with her. She felt like a fool who was intentionally set up to fail. Even though I knew it wasn't so, it was clear that the stretch and the added pressure to perform when she wasn't in the right space was too much.

As tough as the conversation was that day and in the following months, Brooke and I worked together to get her into a role that better suited her needs, supported her recovery, and allowed her to be the professional she wanted to be. This wouldn't have been possible without being sincere about my intentions and what I felt for Brooke.

OPENNESS AND UNDERSTANDING

Natural curiosity has always driven me to understand people; we learn more from our differences when we ask questions and genuinely care about the answer.

I'm often surprised by the breadth and depth of information that strangers reveal in general conversation. Sometimes it can be weird for the person sharing information, especially if they've shared something previously unspoken. When this occurs, I'm quick to reassure them that it's ok and share something personal in return. Despite the occasional weirdness, the sense of relief to get something out is often greater, and it's a privilege to have been given their trust in that moment.

Before writing this book, I'd never really thought about what I said or the method behind making connections – it just happened.

When reflecting on why I am often trusted with people's inner thoughts, I asked my husband Anthony, 'What is it that I do?' His response was, 'It's who you are'. A beautiful compliment, but not helpful for sharing hints and tips with clients and colleagues.

Yes, there are inbuilt personality traits and all that stuff, but who we are is also the result of an experimental adventure with varying degrees of opportunity, confidence, learning, and success as we fumble our way through life.

Even if Anthony had given me a straight answer, I wouldn't have accepted or offered a to-do list for trust. At the start of this book, I suggested you take what is useful and make it your own. That is because I don't believe you can package relationship-building into a hard-wired formula that suits everyone. It needs to be natural, real, and in a style that is still fundamentally yours.

UNEXPECTED INSIGHT

It's funny when you ask a question, and then faith and the universe quickly offer what we need to know. I got the answer to 'What is it that I do?' only a few weeks later from a team member at a Woolworths checkout.

Adam and I had never spoken before, but I had noticed his happy nature and passion for his work. He was always smiling, welcoming and genuinely interested in everyone he met; Adam was a breath of fresh air in the truest sense.

When it was time to serve me, Adam had the same enthusiasm I love seeing in his interactions with every customer. In admiring his service for others, I decided to return his energy and enjoy whatever conversation happened.

I commented that he always greeted people with a wonderful smile as they passed through the checkout. And with attention and tone to signify that I welcomed a meaningful response, I asked how he was going.

Adam's frank reply shocked and saddened me to the point where I still feel a little choked up. I could see that his response surprised him too because, despite his happy demeanour and obvious care and interest in others, Adam said he felt he had lost his life purpose. I immediately experienced his sadness and disappointment. Given the generosity and care radiating from him, it was horrible that he wasn't feeling the energy he gave to everyone else.

I acknowledged how sad and difficult this might be, and he

agreed. I wanted to understand more and offer support, so I asked if there was ever a time when he felt more balanced, and this is where things shifted.

In our five-minute interaction, Adam shared that he had gotten into a rut. His light shone so brightly when he said he used to enjoy painting, and his realisation that he could do this again was beyond words.

By the time Adam had finished scanning and packing my groceries, he'd decided to think about our conversation, maybe look through some photos he had for inspiration, and pick up the brush again.

That day, Adam gave me more than I expected or could have imagined. It was an absolute honour to be trusted with his feelings and hear his unspoken thoughts. I felt joy during Adam's moment of clarity and seeing his face and confidence light up when he identified a way to turn things around.

For both of us, it was a beautiful way to complete an otherwise routine task. It was so automatic, natural, and real that afterwards, I thought deeply about how the conversation, connection and moment of trust came into being.

It was so clear and uplifting that it was worth including in this book. Without realising it, Adam allowed me to fully articulate the HEART+SOUL competencies and combine them with actions for real impact.

Adam and I became friends over multiple grocery packing conversations. Admittedly, it took him a few weeks to pick up a brush, but each time we spoke, he described moving further from the rut.

He encouraged me to share my own challenges and began cheekily holding me to account too. We frequently laughed about our mutual fear of being held accountable and relished the joy of sharing our respective small and big wins. It's wonderful to know that Adam is drawing and painting again.

To this day, Adam's energy is inspiring, and you can see and feel that he really loves serving people. What I love even more is how he positively impacts even the grumpiest of customers. Perhaps that's a result of who he chooses to be.

When we choose to give our HEART+SOUL in everyday interactions, it quickly becomes a natural part of who we are, and we generally become more open.

Being open can create surprising and inspirational connections. The gift you give and the understanding received in return is priceless.

> Being open can create surprising and inspirational connections. The gift you give and the understanding received in return is priceless.

LASTING FOCUS

Having a lasting focus is vital because trust is a long-term goal requiring genuine desire, energy, and considerable effort to build depending on the context. This might be the last of the HEART+SOUL competencies, but it's undoubtedly as important as the others.

Approaching a relationship with the mindset that you're in it for the long term fosters conversations built on mutual respect for personal experience, beliefs, and values.

Even with deadlines and immediate things to do, there is more space to deeply understand what is needed. Not just for now but also for bigger legacy missions. The most successful people (and the ones I have most fun with) approach things in this way because their effort is based on the ongoing value it will provide. This is usually far more sustainable for people and organisations.

Given the level of commitment required to establish trust, it will be useful to consider your ability and desire to do this with the people involved. When you consider all the challenges mentioned in Part One, it's reasonable to expect that sometimes you'll weigh up everything you need to give and decide to build trust elsewhere. If the relationship is one-sided, with you putting in all the effort and receiving little in return, it can feel too tiring and not worth continuing.

Like any relationship worth having, there need to be more ups than downs, and the appreciation for what each person brings must be mutual. If not, you run the risk of resentment creeping in, which isn't healthy for anyone – regardless of how professional and awesome you are at managing your emotional and physical state.

If you can't trust others or feel that you would be selling yourself out by doing so, it's totally ok to walk away. When it comes to relationships, if you fake it, you won't make it!

SOUL THROUGH 'APPRECIATIVE INQUIRY'

Digging deeper into my experiences and thinking, I explored Appreciative Inquiry, which has been found to support behavioural change, improve organisational performance, and foster innovation.[60] I'd heard about it years ago, but as an action-oriented person, I dismissed the theory and didn't give it further thought until recently.

Appreciative Inquiry (Ai) is a way to engage groups of people in self-determined change. It focuses on what's working rather than what's not, and leads to people co-designing their future.[61]

Developed in the early 1990s by David Cooperrider and Suresh Srivastva, Ai can be used in many contexts to partner with and strengthen people. Ai approaches support people with healing, connecting, making sense of things, seeking or obtaining wisdom, and designing and doing what is needed for better outcomes.

The key principles of Ai involve being:

1. **Strengths-based**

   - With questions that amplify strengths and facilitate belief to get things started
   - To maintain momentum, encouragement, and support when things are tough

2. Open to change

- Words create our experience, so what we say needs to be kind
- Our reality is subjective and created through conversations
- We can change our beliefs and actions

3. Founded in experience

- Life is expressed through story and conversation
- We can choose what we study and learn from
- Stories let us process feelings about events and deepen understanding

4. Reflective

- Asking a question creates a shift to be serious, pause and reflect
- Being genuinely curious and interested provokes deeper thought
- Being truthful in our response can change behaviour

5. Outcome and improvement focused

- Imagination drives action
- The more positive and hopeful we are about the future, the more likely action will be taken now to get there. [62] [63]

I've commonly used Ai in service design, organisational change, conflict resolution, and leadership and team coaching in my practice. I wish I'd known about Ai earlier, as it's a great framework for exploring how we can be sincere and open for understanding with a lasting focus.

We've covered a great deal of ground so far, and it's time to put it into action.

When we combine our HEART+SOUL with action, things become meaningful, purposeful, and practical.

REFLECTION

We need to know who we are, what we stand for, and to partner with others.

- What do you appreciate about the people around you?
- What are you thinking, saying, and doing when you're at your best?

The following questions can be useful when you want to support people with SOUL.

- Tell me more?
- What would you do if you had full control of this situation?
- What would be the outcome?
- What can you do for now?
- How can I support you?

PART THREE

DO

CHAPTER 7

MEAN WHAT YOU SAY AND DO IT

Work is meant to be purposeful, where it solves problems, adds value, or does both.

When it comes to professional reputations, it's important to mean what we say and do what we mean. We want people to trust our ability to perform and provide the freedom and autonomy to make the best use of our skills.

People who are trusted model the behaviour they want from others, provide support and are respected leaders who create significant and positive effects for change.[64]

> People who are trusted model the behaviour they want from others, provide support and are respected leaders who create significant and positive effects for change.

Building trust is like riding a bicycle, and every effort counts.

Even if you cruise for a while, at some point, you must keep pedalling, or the journey will come to an end.

Those with deep and enduring relationships don't rest on their past achievements because they realise the importance of maintaining energy and effort with the people they care about.

Knowing we can't be all things to all people, this isn't about constant contact or making sure you lock in regular meetings. It can be casual and as simple as occasionally reaching out on personal things, providing something that may be of interest without agendas or expectations, or checking in on how someone's going while being genuinely interested in the response.

If you already have solid relationships across your organisation, I hope this book encourages you to strengthen and grow them and support others by building their skills.

We've established that creating trust can be easier said than done – particularly if you're in an environment where employees and customers have been burnt in the past.

A further complication occurs when you are (or are perceived as being) connected with individuals, teams or companies who fell short of what was promised or expected.

I distinctly remember one of the first conversations I had with an exec for a large enterprise change. Staring me down, he said, 'You need to earn my trust and prove that I can trust you.'

I was taken aback by his severity, but it was obvious he'd been burnt by whoever was in the role before me. It was also clear that he hadn't recovered from the pain, and two days into the role, through no fault of my own, I'd inherited a bucket load of distrust.

It's one thing to deal with this personally, but quite another if the cynicism is part of larger-scale thinking across multiple teams and employees.

In many organisations, I've met with statements along the lines of 'You're just like all the other.....' and 'We'll wait this out until the next transformation attempt comes along'. Being on the receiving end of such comments can rapidly suck the positivity out of a new role.

Even with the benefit of a baseline Trust Score and understanding from evaluations, culturally embedded distrust is a real challenge. It is even more difficult if you're touted as the new CEO, executive, or specialist, who has come in to change the culture or embed something new. Sometimes it can feel like the pressure is all on you – when it's not.

> Comfort in change comes from knowing what we can influence and control, and who we can depend on to get us through to the other side.

In a complex world of endlessly moving systems in and out of our control, with societal shifts and expectations of continual improvement as business as usual, we're all responsible for adapting to meet needs that are greater than our own.

Even if you're in charge or responsible for delivering, don't assume you must provide all the answers. We're not mind-reading superhumans with infinite wisdom, power, and control. Organisations encompass many people and tribes, all needing to pull together to be successful. We resist change because we don't want to be dragged along or have something done to us.

Comfort in change comes from knowing what we can influence and control, and who we can depend on to get us through to the other side.

WE NEED HELP

I'm stating the obvious when I say that the success of any change rests on the experience and commitment of employees. It's also widely accepted that sustainable all-in efforts are needed, but if people didn't receive any meaningful benefit from their involvement last time, they're unlikely to answer the next call for action.

Recent studies on cynicism about organisational change found that the primary reasons for people's reluctance to be part of any related projects or programs included; distrust about the communicated outcomes, blame towards those leading the change, and a lack of confidence in their ability to do it effectively.[65]

From my exposure to more resistance than eagerness over

the years, I tend to prepare for the worst and be pleasantly surprised when people are truly committed to change. The problem is that it means I can be cynical too. Like many people who've heard the transformational messages and been part of numerous failures, I get the negativity and frustration.

Expectations are founded on life experience, and it can be tempting to transfer what we believe is (or is not) difficult onto others. We need to be mindful that inadvertently projecting our emotions and thoughts blocks our ability to hear other people's perspective of what needs to change, what the changes mean for them, and how to gain genuine benefits.

In asking for help, we can better understand how much effort will be required and the support needed for those impacted to achieve positive outcomes.

Depending on the above, and regardless of size and complexity, organisational change can sometimes be experienced professionally and personally as a crisis.

This response is widespread yet often unspoken among leaders, managers, teams, and individuals who face change. Some situations that can create uncertainty include organisational restructures, role changes, new technology implementations, and service delivery changes.

Never underestimate the effort required for change – even for those who proudly proclaim that they love change. When it comes time to sacrifice something they enjoy, or the work involved turns out to be more difficult than expected, love can turn to hate.

Transformation requires faith in what is yet to be seen or experienced, belief inspires action, and forward movement delivers results.

As an experiential, emotional, rational, and behavioural construct, trust is developed within ourselves and with others in a deeply personal and individual way.

Trust for change requires genuine human connection, clarity, and belief in people's capacity to adapt.

Great leaders know the value of asking for help and leveraging broader experience, particularly in times of uncertainty and crisis. They prioritise conversations to understand what is needed, create calm, and create additional support for people to do things differently, so teams have the opportunity and ability to be successful.

FIND THE DIAMONDS

This trust stuff can be tough if you're in the business of turning around cultures that aren't serving customers or the community as intended and layering any unmanaged business-as-usual stress with the challenges of organisational change. That is unless you find those rare and precious diamond employees looking for an opportunity to do things differently.

> Strength and ownership for positive change and healthy cultures must be built from within.

Fully acknowledging that I'm an external consultant, a popular solution for improving service delivery and changing work cultures is to rely on industry experts. Although this can be useful, large scale outsourcing for transformation generally fails. Externals are also not the experts on your culture. Your employees are.

Strength and ownership for positive change and healthy cultures must be built from within.

Over the last 20 years, there have been multiple studies on the challenges of organisations that rely heavily on external experts and consultants to solve ever-increasing organisational problems. These studies found that employees often feel threatened, devalued and at risk as their skills diminish.[66]

Instead of hiring long-term consultants or contractors, consider the possibility that the function is more suited to permanent employees, who perhaps, with some short-term external guidance or support, can set it up and deliver it ongoing.

Several previous colleagues and I left full-time employment as internal organisational capability advisors because we were tired of the big picture stuff getting given to industry consultants while we were relegated to the sidelines.

Sharing my story with clients often prompts employees to speak up and ask for advice to overcome their frustration and anger at not being engaged for more exciting and challenging work.

Research has shown that managers and employees are significantly more likely to reject externally provided solutions, exert control by withholding valuable information or change recommendations as a form of ego-defence.[67] It also reveals that employee voice and involvement matters, as does co-designing solutions with those who will deliver and receive services.[68, 69, 70]

In advocating to embed permanent employees in the end-to-end activities of programs and projects, sustainability can be baked into solutions as people receive opportunities to leverage their skills for strategic, operational, and professional gain.

> Employees are like diamonds formed from extreme heat, pressure, and the bonding of carbon atoms. With care, they shine with brilliance.

Employees are like diamonds formed from extreme heat, pressure, and the bonding of carbon atoms. With care, they shine with brilliance.

I've stumbled across many rough diamonds, and you probably have too. They're the people who pull you up in the corridor, tell you exactly what they think is wrong with the organisation, and perhaps also tell you what you or someone else needs to do about it. They usually communicate without much finesse. It hits you hard some days, and you'd be forgiven for wishing they would stop complaining.

You could roll your eyes and pass them off as another problem you don't have time for – or acknowledge that they're complaining because they care so much. If you go beneath the surface, ask for more information on what they need to sort the problem and offer support, the conversation often shifts into something more insightful.

By understanding and addressing the causal factors of resistance, outbursts, or underperformance, our effort and ability to work through uncomfortable interactions can go a long way in creating safety and openness for hearing hard truths.

For organisations, the difference between one strategy failure or another that gets delivered as intended is the hard truths that aren't shared or seen.

LISTEN FIRST

If your tendency is towards actions speaking louder than words, you need to remember that charging out in front could see you leaving people behind by acting too soon without adequately understanding the context or the teams' current skills.

In a conversation about leadership, two friends reflected on the value of leading from the back of the pack. It was an unpopular statement at the time because they'd been drilled to lead from the front, but a valid point because it was clear that they needed to slow down to be more effective.

> We need to make sure people are with us before we start running and that the pace is one that everyone can maintain.

We need to make sure people are with us before we start running and that the pace is one that everyone can maintain.

For most of my career, a sense of urgency has resulted in numerous pros and cons. The biggest con is that I create deadlines for the most inane tasks, wonder why I'm stressed, and then realise the pressure was stupidly self-imposed. That might be ok if it only affected me, but being driven can also impact people you work and live with – in ways that aren't always useful.

My inner circle of family, friends, and colleagues have always been brilliant in supporting my growth while keeping me grounded. But the biggest shout-out goes to Lifeline for teaching me the value of really listening and leaning in differently to create and maintain connections for trust.

Lifeline is the most respected and well-known helpline in Australia's crisis support and suicide prevention system. A largely volunteer-based organisation, its trained crisis support workers offer safety for help seekers via a non-linear CARE model to Connect, Attend to needs, Reaffirm and Empower to save lives.

During 2019, Lifeline's success in using a consistent and

supportive process to establish trust with help seekers and build confidence among crisis support teams was demonstrated, with almost one million community members using Lifeline's services either for the first time or as returning help seekers.[71]

For every call answered, crisis support workers experience the value of connecting with people using evidence-based models. Crisis support workers quickly learn that it's obvious to the person on the other end of the phone if their focus slips and they aren't completely present. Help seekers always have control of the conversation, and they will pull up (or worse, hang up) if crisis support workers don't provide what they need. During training and my year on the phones, I learned it was never about me, my opinions, expectations, or timeframes.

Remember that the person you want to build trust with determines the distance and pace of the journey.

With absolute gratitude and humility, my experiences at Lifeline taught me what was needed to pull this book together. On a far more meaningful level, the training and support I received as a crisis support worker saved the lives of strangers and some of my closest friends.

> Remember that the person you want to build trust with determines the distance and pace of the journey.

The ability to listen for understanding is relevant for non-crisis situations, too. Perhaps if we did this more often, we could prevent a great deal of crisis and be kinder as a community.

Just like my conversation with Adam at the grocery check-out, trust conversations can occur in any context. It's surprising how often seemingly random conversations can turn into life-changing moments of warmth, clarity, and hope. What I love about connected conversations is that by giving, you also receive.

WORK WITH TEAMS

Our beliefs, attitudes, communication and behaviour at work significantly impact those around us. In referencing the earlier mentioned challenges for trust, people who successfully navigate these give their HEART+SOUL to achieve amazing things.

The Foundation for Indigenous Sustainable Health (FISH) embodies HEART+SOUL. An inspiring Western Australian organisation, FISH, focuses on real and lasting change to break 'generational cycles of poverty, trauma and engagement with the justice system'.

With acknowledgement and respect to Aboriginal and Torres Strait Islander people as the first peoples of Australia and the traditional owners of the land, FISH knows that 'for lasting change, projects need to be by Aboriginal people, for Aboriginal people. Buildings and programs need to belong to the place and the people.'[72]

Learning is supported, and challenges are worked through in partnership, with reverence for people's authority, wisdom and insight. FISH holistically co-designs, delivers, and develops lasting community programs to provide housing, life skills, personal development, and creative initiatives.

By maintaining a positive focus on what is possible, connecting with people and country, and working side-by-side, community goals are achieved.

It's exciting to see photos and stories on LinkedIn and their website (www.fish.asn.au) about what they and the community to do. Whether intentional or not, they use an evidence-based approach for success. For your organisation, the ability to do as FISH has done is vital for implementing change and enabling transformation.[73]

A great place to start is understanding why things need to change, knowing what needs doing differently and with whom. People often get stuck getting clear on how to work with other teams and inspiring action.

When overcoming inertia, it's easy to overemphasise the importance of speed and forget that establishing relationships and progressing an outcome requires care.

This can be particularly prevalent in programs and project work

> When overcoming inertia, it's easy to overemphasise the importance of speed and forget that establishing relationships and progressing an outcome requires care.

where people are pushed to turn things around within tight and often unreasonable timeframes – often to a point where speed becomes more important than quality. Such a focus can drive panicked and cringe-worthy behaviours from consultants and employees alike.

Think of a pushy salesperson who is desperate to take your money, delivers a minimal viable product, and then approaches as many of your friends as possible to sell more before anyone realises that the outcome isn't what is needed.

I've worked with multiple organisations and have seen this approach fail rapidly. It wasn't that the people were horrible; it was more that they were pushed to prove, sell, and deliver a product rather than connecting with why it was needed and who it was for.

What's worse is that these pressures aren't always external; they can also come from managers and executives disconnected from operational realities.[74]

> When forced to prove ourselves, we can lose sight of who we're supposed to be serving and why we're there in the first place.

Whether you're internal or external, there's often much focus on needing to prove our worth – particularly if the primary delivery focus is on time, on budget, and at all costs. Those costs are usually the inability to deliver a quality product or service, or worse, at the expense of people's well-being.

I've faced pressure to force through a solution and stepped away because it didn't feel right, and it wasn't. No one likes to be pushed too hard, receive something that doesn't meet their needs, or be driven to exhaustion in the pursuit of obtaining it.

When forced to prove ourselves, we can lose sight of who we're supposed to be serving and why we're there in the first place.

Sure, change can happen by smashing things through to implementation, but the quality of what is delivered often isn't there, and neither are the people to support and embed the change. Hence the typical gap between strategy and sustainable delivery of genuine benefits.

Even if achieving change is a non-negotiable, without applying what we're covering in this book, engagement strategies and change readiness activities without meaningful consultation and involvement in their design and implementation can come off as arrogant, aggressive and insulting.

It's better to be known as someone who takes time to understand the experience of others, dares to shine a light in dark corners, and cares to get it right, rather than someone who rams through poor quality solutions leaving behind a trail of destruction and disgruntled people who can't deliver.

> The most valuable activities for trust involve partnering with people as highly capable individuals and teams.

In *The Trusted Advisor*,[75] Maister, Green and Galford identified the value of respect, warmth, and promoting other people's experience. Their book highlights that building trust is not about us. It's about being in service and enabling others to excel and own achievements by being professionally inclusive.

The most valuable activities for trust involve partnering with people as highly capable individuals and teams.

3C MODEL FOR TRUST

It's imperative to build the foundational competencies for trust, but the kicker is living them with authenticity and realism.

Providing space for people to share truths and work through challenges is never about running through and completing checklists. While acknowledging that models are useful in contextualising complex concepts, trust is not just about applying a methodology.

Without HEART+SOUL, conversations can feel process-driven, theoretical, routine, and fake.

If you don't genuinely understand and empathise with the needs of those directly impacted by your changes, don't expect any investment in strategies and plans that didn't leverage the breadth, depth, and knowledge of their experience.

I considered several outcome-focused models[76] to practically apply HEART+SOUL, that, at first glance, appeared linear or stepped, even if this wasn't my intention.

How we engage, interact, and build relationships is more fluid, with lots of motion in and around topics or experiences until we reach some form of mutual understanding, clarity, and commitment with others.

Appreciating that sometimes relationships need to go back and forth, I considered feedback loops and improvement cycles, but none connected.

For HEART+SOUL alignment, I created the 3C model for trust. My daughter Hayley loves the calming design and alliteration because it's easy to remember. My clients and I like it because it's simple and it works. The 3Cs are:

- Connect
- Clarify
- Commit

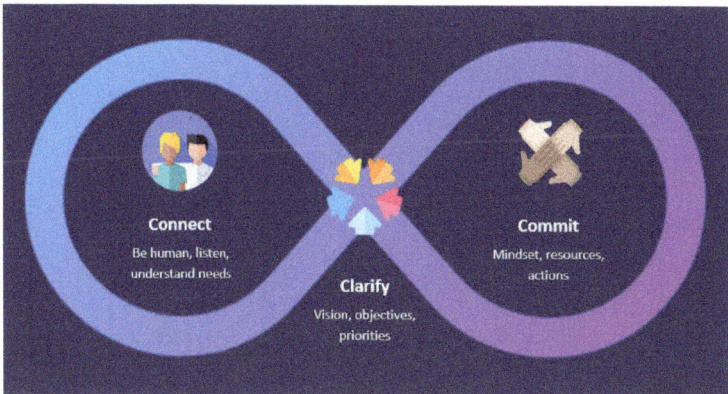

Figure 6: The 3Cs

This model works because it incorporates the emotional, cognitive, and behavioural components for making improvements – individually and with others.

We'll go through the detail in our last couple of chapters, but for now, here is a summary:

Connect

Be human. Listen. Understand needs.

To connect, be authentic with who you are, what you care about, and why the person you're listening to matters.

If you need to tell people to trust you or announce that you're a leader or an expert, it's a sure sign that you have more work to do.

Connecting is the feeling we get when we're fully interested in someone or something. It's not about the exact words or what you do; it's about how you feel during and long after the interaction has occurred.

This happens when all the HEART+SOUL competencies are fully engaged so that those you want to partner with know that you're with them and will behave in their best interests.

Connection is about being. It is for others to decide whether to consider and accept your offer of trust in them.

When you connect, it means that you get it because you've attended to their needs and felt what is going on for them. You have understood their perspective and value and accepted them for who they are.

Clarify

Vision. Objectives. Priorities.

If we want or need to transform organisational culture, a team or just ourselves, it's easy to get caught in the current emotion, churn, or volume of work, and be crippled by stuff that is simply getting in the way.

Organisations are full of old systems, emotions, and expectations of maintaining business as usual – all of which scream so loud that it can be hard to think. To be serious about working in ways that better serve us in the long run, we need rational perspective to accurately assess what is important, what we can delegate, what we need to stop doing, and what must be done differently.

When everything around us is noisy, we need strategies to slow down, consider alternative perspectives, and determine which efforts will produce the best return.

With clarity comes clear direction and priorities for action. When you've got this, it's because you've been able to remove or reduce noise, focus on what matters most, and create a plan for action to eliminate, delegate, and do what matters.

Commit

Mindset. Resources. Actions.

If your individual, team and organisational efforts aren't aligned and committed as one, the results will be random, with duplication of effort. The experience will be frustrating, painful, and with little to no return on investment.

A commitment must be a holistic partnership, first with yourself and then with others across the organisational system.

Regardless of how much everyone nods and agrees with the vision, their ability to have skin in the game and feel the benefit of doing so is the difference between a great idea and people doing what they say they will.

> Leaders don't seek out power or influence over others, they seek the contentment found in growing people, so everyone can realise and wield their full and unique potential.

Leaders don't seek out power or influence over others, they seek the contentment found in growing people, so everyone can realise and wield their full and unique potential.

People commit because they have made a decision with discipline, consistency, and trust.

REFLECTION

- What do you feel about the changes?
- What do these changes mean for you?
- What is creating noise and draining energy?
- How can you reduce noise and create calm for clarity?
- How committed are you to the work ahead?
- Who do you need to connect and be professionally inclusive with?

CHAPTER 8

CONNECT

Trust is a complex mix of multiple feelings, thoughts and behaviours. You can't fake genuine.

THE JOURNEY IS THEIRS

Keep in mind that change at work often involves a loss of control, calm, direction or focus. As Dr Adam Fraser says, 'Innovation is not fun! Innovation is a process rich in vulnerability, and it is inherently uncomfortable. If it feels good, it's not innovation'.[77]

> Trust is a complex mix of multiple feelings, thoughts and behaviours. You can't fake genuine.

For example, work changes can involve losing credit for work already done, enjoyment of previous or current work that will be given to someone else, losing team-mates, colleagues, convenience, or location, among other things which might not be obvious.

Loss always produces an emotional response, and these

responses can be more extreme in some people than others. For this reason, the emotional stages of grief are often referred to in training and support programs as the change curve.

Connecting is about respecting the emotions of change by offering the HEART+SOUL for trust.

Elisabeth Kübler-Ross and David Kessler's book *On Grief and Grieving* identified five key stages people go through when experiencing loss. Progress occurs through the non-linear stages of denial, anger, depression, bargaining, and acceptance.[78]

Leaders enable safety by facilitating self-management with questions for people to identify options, provide confidence for a decision, and support for implementing solutions. To do this, connecting, both generally and in times of uncertainty, requires accepting and sitting comfortably with emotions while supporting people to work through change.

A common challenge for connecting in stressful situations is that focusing on others is intensive and may take more time than you have in the moment or are willing to give later. It can be hard to fight the urge to jump in with the solution and accept the other person's style and pace without making assumptions.

> For perspective and insight, we need to have patience and be open.

For perspective and insight, we need to have patience and be open.

To connect, we must truly be the message people need to hear. This requires us to be authentic with who we are, why we care, and why the person we're listening to is capable and important.

Earlier, we touched on Lifeline's CARE model and the effectiveness of this for help seekers. The most important element of CARE is the crisis support worker's ability to connect.

> To connect, we must truly be the message people need to hear. This requires us to be authentic with who we are, why we care, and why the person we're listening to is capable and important.

The same is true for creating and nurturing any relationship. We seek to be heard, understood, and accepted for who we are, and for this to happen, we first pay attention to and are influenced by what we feel.

If you're practising servant leadership, deeper vulnerabilities will be revealed, and it takes time, patience, people's trust, and their belief in outcomes that are yet to be experienced.

Under the Law of Reciprocity, it's common to find that the support and energy we give return at some point and in-kind, so consider the impact of your energy on others.[79]

If we think of ourselves as service providers, the best experiences from an employee and customer perspective will likely be genuine, adaptive to people's needs, and allow the freedom to be respectfully honest about what can and can't be delivered. Any interactions that seem scripted, flat, over-expressive, or insincere can be jarring, create cynicism, and result in more cautious behaviour.[80]

When influencing and supporting others, the greater the uncertainty and need for cultural change, the more the likelihood of resistance, emotional reactions, and interpersonal conflicts. In these situations, we need the other person's permission before offering advice.

Numerous studies have found that the most stable and consistent leadership style for encouraging employees to discuss what they're really thinking and feeling is that of servant leadership.[81]

Regardless of the urgency or importance of the message, we need to remember that it's not about us; it's about serving others in the hope that they will also listen, understand, and work with us.

The ability to be in service requires tapping in emotionally to what people are experiencing to promote partnership and collaboration for improvement. Before putting plans in place and asking for people's commitment to a cause, we must first attend to their needs, feel what they are feeling, understand their experience, and accept their perspective.

Looking at this more closely from a team and organisational perspective, our ability to create connections and partnerships is the difference between success and failure.

Attend

There is mutual benefit and power in giving someone your full attention by staying in the moment, being still and listening to what they need.

It seems obvious, but when everyone is busy and working through competing priorities and deadlines, we can be so preoccupied about whether the information we're receiving will help or hinder that we miss crucial messages and unspoken signals.

It's often said that silence is golden, and I've certainly been guilty of saying silence equals agreement. But if you don't check your assumptions, this could also be the sound of quiet dissent and people planning their exit.

Attending to others means being generous with our time, energy and focus, to understand what is unsaid.

When you're under pressure, promoting extra effort might seem unrealistic and counterintuitive. However, if you get it right the first time, you won't have to hear the story over and over to achieve understanding and partnership later. So, consider connecting efforts as a worthy investment.

> Attending to others means being generous with our time, energy and focus, to understand what is unsaid.

Alternatively, when people are caught in a loop and keep

repeating the same message, it's because they feel others don't get it or that goals are misaligned.

After a while, if people keep hitting a brick wall, they'll shut down and stop talking. This is where interpersonal and organisational risk creeps in. It's why we've covered the challenges for trust throughout this book and why silence is not always golden.

If you need to prevent risks from developing into issues, creating safety for others to tell you often comes by playing back the emotion you are hearing, seeing, or sensing to validate what is real for them first.

An important distinction is that attending isn't problem-solving; it's about sitting with whatever someone is going through at that moment.

I relearn this from my daughter and son whenever they come home from a horrible and infuriating day at work or school, and I go into fix-it mode instead of being present. I've missed the point often enough for them both to remind me with, 'Mum I just need you to listen while I vent' before they kick into describing what is going on. It's part of their problem-solving process. When I shut up, they become capable of figuring things out for themselves.

> Show up, silence your internal dialogue, and be fully present for someone else.

Whether at home or work, when you care and see people suffering, it's hard not to jump straight in and try to save them. But in doing so, we're not attending to what the person telling the story needs at that moment. We're focussed on removing our discomfort in hearing about it, and not trusting their ability to get it sorted.

Show up, silence your internal dialogue, and be fully present for someone else.

Feel

Depending on whether you're more of a connector for facts or feelings, this may be something that comes with practise and the patience I mentioned earlier.

Whether we like it or not, we're emotional beings. Our differences are more about our levels of awareness and managing them for ourselves and others.

I've mentioned a few of my experiences in volatile work cultures, and despite being someone who connects easily with emotional cues, this does not make life easy.

From an incredibly early age, my son Hayden has been challenged by this. He is both blessed and cursed in that he has always deeply and intensely felt others' experience. It's an observation numerous teachers have shared over the years because it has impressed them, and in the name of justice, has been at the root of a few schoolyard scuffles.

As adults, our broader life experiences attest to our growth, but I admit that when emotions are running high, there are times when I'd love nothing more than to hulk smash something. The thing is, it's the behaviour and the context that can bring out a monster in all of us. Our response is what matters most.

For an extreme example of managing thoughts, emotions and volatility, read Australian Victorian Cross (VC) recipient Mark Donaldson's autobiography *The Crossroad*. In contrast to receiving Australia's highest award for bravery, Donaldson offers incredible insight into his heartbreaking and self-destructive life leading up to becoming a member of the elite Special Air Service Regiment (SASR or SAS) and the challenges he overcame to 'become something bigger or better'.[82]

Emotions happen – they're not a choice, but we can learn to manage and control how we express them. Keep in mind that unmanaged highly emotional states don't support creating great solutions. We'll get to that in the last two chapters, but for now...

Listen with complete care so that the person speaking feels calm, comfortable, heard, and valued during the conversation and long afterwards.

To work with what people are feeling, it's useful to accept the feeling for what it is, create the space to turn the volume down to a manageable level, focus on the outcome that is needed, and offer a meaningful way for people to express feelings to support deeper thinking.

Understand

In seeking to understand, we encourage and support broader perspectives and foster collaboration on solutions by respecting others' voices.

Be curious about the other person's perspective, what the situation means for them and how it impacts their world.

On the flipside of creating positive experiences with HEART+SOUL, fatigue can easily creep in if we're constantly giving to others, such as working on a help desk, delivering community services, or in other roles involving direct contact with people needing support.[83, 84]

Understanding comes from time spent training, on the playing field, and in doing the work.

If you're not responsible for using the plans, policies, processes, and equipment to get the job done, respect that although you might set the direction, navigate, and guide the aircraft, you're certainly not the one flying it.

It's more important to know what people do when you're not looking than relying on formal interactions and reports for

> If you're not responsible for using the plans, policies, processes, and equipment to get the job done, respect that although you might set the direction, navigate, and guide the aircraft, you're certainly not the one flying it.

understanding. This matters even more if your organisation has red flags of distrust, underperformance, and disengagement, which generally occur when people don't feel that something is meaningful, safe, or possible for them to perform at their best.[85]

No one wants to deliver or receive poor quality services, so appealing to people's better natures and desires to live up to their code of values and ethics is far more useful than punishing people further.[86, 87]

To assure them that we get it, share a personal vulnerability or experience that is unseen or unexpected. This could mean explaining that your concerns about risk are similar to theirs. Allowing people to see our humanity first is like saying it's ok not to be ok, that we have concerns too, and we're looking for people to be real with us.

If you're unsure of the benefits of revealing vulnerabilities, consider the last time you felt safe to drop your mask and speak freely. Chances are, it was a relief and opened the door for others to do the same.

Accept

Trust that you're adding and receiving incredible value by purposefully listening for understanding and accepting the information and insights offered to you.

Things shift all the time, and if we don't think a change will benefit us, chances are we'll resist it. Depending on what we think we'll lose, our emotions about events are likely to be negative. The breadth and depth of this depend on the context and magnitude of the impact.

I prefer the term 'acceptance' when needing to adopt something I'm not happy about. This is because I still hold power to disagree and not like it. Acceptance means I'm choosing to work with change to a point where I'll be ok – or if I can't be ok, then I create alternatives to adapt and become less uncomfortable.

> Trust that you're adding and receiving incredible value by purposefully listening for understanding and accepting the information and insights offered to you.

As covered earlier, we don't choose what we feel or when – they're just a response. How we manage them is up to us. Before that, though, we need the ability to express emotions in a way that enables others to share without judgment.

The benefits of accepting what is happening right now:

- Demonstrate an inner calm, strength in who you are, and what you offer in giving your complete and undivided attention
- Provide validation that their experience matters
- Allow people to feel unconditionally valued for who they are as a person and what they're trying to achieve, even if the result isn't optimal
- Offer space for a deeper understanding of what is happening, why, and its impact on people.

TRANSFORMATION IS INTERNAL

With so much focus on organisations becoming customer-centric and improving the Customer Experience (CX), organisational surveys regarding the Employee Experience (EX) can sometimes become a secondary focus.

As mentioned in earlier chapters, real problems occur when EX becomes a lower priority or is completely ignored because EX feeds CX. We've all experienced moments when we're not feeling the best for whatever reason, and we're adult enough to admit that when we're flat, our performance suffers too.

Even if we're lucky enough for others not to notice our disengagement, if we don't look after ourselves, the wheels of whatever we're driving will eventually start falling off.

Just as robots need care and maintenance to keep working, if you or the people around you are creaky and need oil, perhaps it's time to receive a little love. The ability to receive is just as important as giving because people often like to help and feel honoured when they can.

Organisationally, we need our fingers on the pulse to check that systems are working as best they can. When used with integrity and a genuine commitment to understand and serve, employee surveys provide great insights into what people think about the organisation. They also identify where deeper unfiltered intelligence, beyond what executives and middle managers might formally report, is needed to drive meaningful improvements and seek additional benefits.

Employee surveys are indeed a snapshot in time. It's also fair to say that if you're looking at something more than six months old, the report may not accurately describe the current state of a team's culture. A review of what has changed since the findings can be invaluable for knowing where to start now.

A deep understanding of employee experiences and their impacts is vital if you've chosen to lead, influence, enable and support change. If there haven't been any measurable improvements or interventions beyond training and communication to address pain points in the last survey, any anecdotally reported gains could be superficial, unsustainable, or too small scale for larger impact and benefit. Without action and intelligence, the culture could be worse.

Silence is deadly

The cultures that most disturb me are those where people say nothing at all – they just look beaten, and you can't wait to wash off the heavy and miserable vibe. I wrote earlier about silent dissent, but at a deeper level, this is where people exist at work in a state of learned helplessness.

The concept of learned helplessness is where people are conditioned to expect unavoidable pain, suffering and discomfort.[88] Once reached, this state significantly and negatively impacts their emotions, thinking, behaviours, and they're far from inspired or ready for change. In this state, people believe that whatever they try won't result in a more positive outcome.

A few years ago, I worked with a blended team of permanent

171

employees and long-term contractors. It was clear they were suffering because I could feel and see it when I walked the floor.

In understanding their business, I was excited about the opportunity to work with them because I believed in and cared about what they wanted to achieve.

To ensure my expectations were grounded, my closest colleague warned, 'Be careful; that's the place where good people go to die.' He wasn't wrong – the area had a horrible reputation, and the teams were doing a crazy amount of churn work that didn't add sustainable value. They were usually engaged too little and too late for any work in which they could make a significant positive impact.

One team member described that they were caught in multiple negative infinity loops. They looked more like work zombies gazing silently into their computers than people who could make a real difference to the organisation and its customers. They weren't empowered to make changes, and the work was boring and uninspiring. What they delivered was never heard or understood within the organisation's performance and governance structure, and even their Branch Head didn't understand their value.

The team members were so miserable they didn't talk to each other much anymore and had stopped collaborating across smaller teams. They stayed within their lanes, operated in silos, and what I saw and felt was a culture of existence.

They had experienced a few wins here and there, but that was purely from individual levels of care and dogged persistence rather than support from their Executive. As a result, the team struggled for traction to deliver more productive and innovative work towards the organisation's desired outcomes.

Working in the area had sucked the life out of otherwise clever and creative people. A few were described as aggressive, non-team players and underperformers.

Sadly, this team represents many I've worked with – you may have been involved with such a group yourself. It's also fair to say that no-one wants to be associated with this scenario.

Over the remaining chapters, I'll weave in the story of an Employee Experience (EX) team that managed to turn things around with HEART+SOUL and the 3Cs. If you know a team like this, it can work for your organisation too.

Customers can't always be first

Let me set the scene for the EX team. Generally, at the group and team level, executives, managers, and employees didn't share much information among themselves. Robust discussion of alternative views was regarded as unhealthy conflict, and collaboration without permission was unwelcome rebellion.

> By focussing on the outside, we can miss the insights and opportunities immediately available, usually at a significantly reduced cost.

Adaptive thinking and behaviours

beyond putting out fires to address immediate customer pain, or doing anything outside of defined areas of expertise, was risky business professionally and personally.

There was so much pressure on the larger organisation from angry external groups and customers pushing for better and more reliable services, that internal feedback from the employees responsible for delivery had become a significantly lower priority.

By focussing on the outside, we can miss the insights and opportunities immediately available, usually at a significantly reduced cost.

> Employee capability and organisational performance improve when active engagement occurs through open and unfiltered conversation with people who understand the root cause of issues.

Executives had the results of an earlier culture survey, which, if used appropriately, could have opened the door to discussions with employees on what was needed, why, and how things could be better for everyone.

If they had prioritised and invested in building more informal relationships by doing simple things like regularly walking the floor to hear from employees more casually, they would have received valuable intelligence on how to prevent multiple issues impacting customers.

Employee capability and organisational performance improve when active engagement occurs through open and unfiltered conversation with people who understand the root cause of issues.

It provides the freedom to identify, learn through experimentation, and work with others on solutions aimed at delivering higher value.[89]

If the effort doesn't produce the desired outcome, at least they can provide compelling and evidence-based business cases to support different approaches or further investment.

Know what is real

To their credit, the EX team had made numerous and varied attempts to partner with others for the greater good, only to be squashed and pushed back into maintaining business as usual and just keeping the lights on.

They found it infuriating to be disempowered over things they knew would make things better internally and externally for the organisation.

From the outside, it was incredibly sad to see passionate and talented people lose themselves and the skills they brought to the organisation. What they wanted to do, and could have done before, was now just theory.

During an interview, one usually silent employee told me candidly that I wasn't the first consultant who had interviewed them, and he'd seen many over the years. He hoped that things would be different but said he wasn't more involved publicly because – despite my best intentions – he accepted that things probably wouldn't change.

As with my earlier recollection of being outlasted, he believed it wasn't worth investing extra energy only to be disappointed yet again.

His pain was profound, and if you were to picture him as a wounded animal who'd lost the will to live, you'd be on the mark as to how he came across at work. I imagined a time where he would have been a high performer, speaking up and even getting angry for not being heard. Now he was just resigned, clocking in and out each day to get paid.

I empathised deeply with him and others in the team who shared similar grim views. They were right – there can be a massive gap between great ideas and the real world.

PREACHING VS PRACTISING

Over more than 20 years as a permanent employee in the private and public sectors, I've witnessed countless external experts impressing senior leadership teams with organisational strategies and plans that never come to full or even partial fruition.

Some of the best roles I've had were providing internal HR and business improvement consulting and coaching, but often the advice of corporates and externals was valued more than that of those needing to bring the strategies to life.

In the spirit of full transparency, I was a significant author and advocate for a strategy and plan that was so awesome it was rolled out as mandatory training across the organisation. It was a key contributor in winning an award for the organisation.

The plan was brilliant – until implemented in a non-corporate setting, where it wasn't operationally viable because it was impractical, with an overkill from a training perspective, and no staffing allocation or budget for areas working 24/7 shifts to attend.

Even more ridiculous was that I'd fought so hard to make it happen and didn't see the error until I had to make it so myself. After slapping my forehead, begging forgiveness, and working more closely with operational areas, the plan was significantly reworked to be relevant and suitable. But my naivety was painful, creating unnecessary stress for numerous areas that were already under the pump. It was an incredibly valuable lesson to learn.

When a strategy isn't connected to operational reality, the people who are responsible and best placed to deliver it suffer and withdraw.

> When a strategy isn't connected to operational reality, the people who are responsible and best placed to deliver it suffer and withdraw.

You've read enough to know that I like rolling my sleeves up and working side-by-side with teams to fix stuff, but it's far better to provide services that inspire and enable people, so things aren't broken in the first place.

The EX team had a similar goal; with a deep understanding of business issues and impacts and great ideas about how things could improve, they wanted to be part of the solution. They frequently volunteered and provided evidence-based recommendations, but permission to play was rarely or never granted. On occasion, they could get involved, their scope was extremely limited – and mostly when it was too late.

This wasn't just a problem for this team, though. Across the organisation, permanent employees were mostly responsible for supporting or fixing whatever external program or project teams had delivered in isolation. Entire departments were often left to operationalise or roll out solutions or recommendations that were so removed from reality that they were difficult or impossible to implement and sustain.

Acknowledging that the team's skills were deteriorating through lack of use, we agreed that for any chance of success, they would have to be part of, own and be accountable for any proposed ideas and interventions to improve the situation. Together, we needed to build from the ground up.

It took time to build relationships, and what I'm offering in *Connect* is the tip of the iceberg. I'm also aware that allowing others to set the pace of conversations might require a crazy amount of patience, but the information shared in connecting is vital to *Clarify* what is needed, and *Commit* to outcomes.

REFLECTION

- Who do you need to understand?
- What matters most to individuals and teams?
- How will you be of service to their needs?

CHAPTER 9

CLARIFY

'The common differentiator between adaptive and chaotic teams is trust.'

– Grant Chisnall[90]

Not framing up the problem needing to be solved is like lifting a rock and seeing hundreds of cockroaches scurry out while hoping to kill them all at once with a single shot of insect spray.

I've met managers who take great pride in their team's skills to survive and their ability to save them from being pulled apart by Senior Executives who don't get it.

Overcoming knocks and being resilient can be worn as a badge of honour. Still, despite the occasionally brave faces, those in this space for extended periods or under recurring threat can become unproductive, deeply miserable, and tend to accept their existence as paying the bills and business as usual.

In situations like this, people can easily get caught up in

defending the status quo. Losing sight of their importance to larger outcomes makes motivation plummet. The risk is even greater when service becomes less about quality and more about putting out fires.

The EX team attributed most of their knockbacks and confusion to the way their team was established, changed over time, and where they were in the organisation. I largely agreed with their assessment and added a lack of clarity, investment, support to develop their initial skills, and the freedom to meaningfully enhance what they did was also an issue. When I described this to the team, a relieved sigh was followed by an animated, unanimous, and loud 'YES!'

Their inability to articulate the basics of why the organisation needed them, and the impact of not leveraging their knowledge and experience, was a massive problem. Without communicating the benefits of what they wanted to offer clearly and with conviction, people could not understand their value strategically or operationally. With a looming organisational restructure in play, they were at risk of being considered irrelevant and becoming disbanded.

The crazy thing was that they were part of a Group that was failing on a massive scale. This was particularly evident in feedback from employees and customers across other agencies who found it frustrating to use the organisation's products and services for their most basic needs.

Given the Group's long history of poor performance, there was significant external distrust in the organisation's ability to deliver fit-for-purpose services. It also didn't help that they had no clear service catalogue for orders and purchases.

Unsurprisingly, for customers outside of the Group to maintain business operations, non-integrated, shadow products and services popped up everywhere as other areas bought and developed their own solutions. These were not just for area-specific requirements but also enterprise standard solutions.

The Group was rapidly becoming irrelevant as people at all levels of the enterprise worked around them.

The larger strategy to become more customer-centric was called out in a big picture plan, but there was a serious lack of understanding and experience in bringing this to life.

They needed a large-scale cultural shift from where the Group was, to where it needed to be.

Both employee and customer expertise were vital to reframe thinking, challenge existing practices, change priorities, processes, and behaviours, and fully commit to a new approach if they hoped to enable the organisation to deliver strategically.

The entire Group was in stormy political waters. There was plenty of energy to drive continuous improvement, but unfortunately for the specialists who could have facilitated and supported this, messages weren't getting through as intended. It seemed that key executives weren't ready to hear or act either.

In the absence of senior executive partnership with operational areas and considering the emotions and uncertainty of upcoming organisational changes, the best that could be done for the EX team was to work on their internal efficiencies and hope for a larger flow-on effect.

To maintain a strategic view, an inclusive partnership was agreed between the team and surrounding supporters. The goal was to co-design a new service model to better position and promote higher-value and lower-cost services.

Although the team couldn't be sure whether people would accept a more ambitious service offer, they trusted themselves and each other. Offering what they knew and felt was right for the Group's employees and customers was enough to boost their spirits.

In fairness to the non-supporters and naysayers, sometimes people can't consume the information that supports change. When overwhelmed by what is not working, it is difficult to cut through the noise and know where to start. You don't want to burn people by trying to tackle everything at once – especially if it's to drive something different or new.

> Having clarity is like putting the windscreen wipers on when it rains.

Having clarity is like putting the windscreen wipers on when it rains.

Grant Chisnall, the founder of the company Left of Boom[91], is an expert at preparing for and managing crises, with experience that spans military and civilian contexts. He puts trust down to people leaning into the problem, working collaboratively, and embracing opportunities to learn and adapt.[92]

The EX team's main problem was their inability to clearly articulate their value for others. Instead of leaning into this together, they had splintered and were so busy putting out fires that they had lost the real reason they existed. The team needed to work collaboratively to; remove or reduce noise, focus on value, create a plan to learn and adapt, and deliver immediate and sustainable benefits towards the bigger picture.

BE CLEAR ON WHAT YOU OFFER

What does success look like? It's an obvious first question when it comes to visualising what organisations need to achieve. Despite most organisations or companies having what they believe is a clear vision statement, they rarely come to fruition due to getting lost in translation.

As far as developing visions that involve others – if you're telling, you're selling.

People don't like to be sold; they need to identify why changes are essential and how they will make a difference. After all, they'll be the ones responsible for the lion's share of the work to get there.

Interestingly, our EX team had a shared vision, but individuals and other teams lacked an understanding of what was needed, why, and the time and collective effort required to have a greater and more sustainable impact.

As with my previous failed attempts at value-adding before having a clearer understanding or relationship with people I needed to partner with, the EX team often came across as overly passionate, full-on, and offering too much, too soon.

If you took the time to unpack it, their operational intent was brilliant and aligned with the strategic vision. But for the managers and executives they were pitching to, it was like suggesting a marathon when people were still on the couch and didn't own a pair of runners. It didn't feel right, the timing was wrong, and it all seemed too hard.

Sadly, the team was not alone, as other teams across the Group were experiencing similar challenges.

More broadly, vision statements fail when:

- There is insufficient understanding of the organisation's existing services, how they are connected, why they're essential for people, and why they need to evolve.
- The vision for the organisation is inconsistent with the activities to improve the employee experience in delivering services.
- The associated plans are so high-level that they offer no meaning for delivery areas that must create and adhere to plans, policies, and procedures for what and how things need to be done.
- There is inadequate flexibility and investment in the people, skills, capability, resources, and support to achieve it.[93, 94]

Clear visions provide compelling benefits for change by identifying the expected return on investment for the work ahead. Motivation comes from people's ability to visualise and feel what success will mean for them.

Without clarity on what needs to be achieved, how they will be supported, and the benefits that will follow, people will keep doing what they've always done or wait for direction. Even if it's churn work, people would rather be 'busy' than bored.

To create clarity, it helps to know your purpose and how you can provide a meaningful service for others.

> To create clarity, it helps to know your purpose and how you can provide a meaningful service for others.

Matt Church, the founder of Thought Leaders Business School,[95] offers a blunt yet effective approach to defining what you offer by answering three questions from the perspective of the people you want to engage:

- Who are you?
- What do you do?
- Why should I care?

When pulled together, it's known as an elevator pitch. It describes your ability to offer information clearly and purposefully in the time it takes to get in and out of an elevator. Not surprisingly, it's important to know and believe this about ourselves before expecting others to get it. But in our haste to get the message out, we often forget to answer the last question, which focusses on 'What is in it for them?'

When individuals and teams aren't performing to potential, it's because they can't answer all three questions with conviction.

An even greater challenge occurs when members of the same team tell you different things, and what they say doesn't seem to line up with the collective effort and outcomes needed.

If this is happening, people are working in isolation. What and how they deliver shows little understanding or consideration of the flow-on impacts or benefits for the organisation or others.

Being clear about what you offer isn't about embarking on a fancy and expensive branding and communications strategy. I'm referring to what we say in conversation that attracts or repels people.

It's the real and natural things that roll off our tongues with little effort or thought because it's just who we are, how we operate, and what we deliver. These are what we need to leverage to create connections and a desire to work together.

Our ability to be clear on what we offer, with the confidence that it's useful and serves a purpose, is hard-wired to our productivity. If we feel that what we do doesn't matter, why bother? When we're encouraged by the responses to our offer, we'll lean in and work to give more.

It's tempting to rush in and save the day when things are

burning, and you've been tasked with putting out the fires, but taking on too much is the fast track to burn out. We've heard the phrase 'Don't work long and hard, work smart!' but how we do so can be tricky, and depending on the chaos you're in can seem nearly impossible.

FRAME CHALLENGES

Emotions add additional complexity and noise to everyday issues. Breaking through the noise by systemically framing what needs to be done creates calm and clarity for action.

Leaders know how to cut through distractions, prioritise and focus efforts on what matters based on people's skills, the return and benefits expected from the investment and the effort required.

Knowing the components of the game and skills of the team allows for easier coaching on what is needed for the outcome.

> Knowing the components of the game and skills of the team allows for easier coaching on what is needed for the outcome.

An Australian study by Pignata, Boyd, Winefield and Provis involved 10,883 employees across 13 organisations. They found that stress reduces significantly, and people perform more effectively when they feel ownership of their role. It's especially so when they know the expectations and boundaries, have a level of control in their work, flexibility in how they do it, can access opportunities for promotion, and feel skilled and resourced professionally and personally to perform.[96]

For clarity, we also need to understand the challenges, blockers and noise that could inhibit our performance for the larger purpose:

- Consider the employee and customer perspective.
- Enable and support honest discussion about the challenges, risks, and issues.
- Unpack what you suspect to be the root causes.
- Respect boundaries and set expectations by communicating that you are only interested in solving what the evidence and the people involved state is the most important.[97]
- Consider the broader process and service flow and how this fits with the larger organisational system.[98]
- Identify and validate across multiple disciplines to ensure adequate and holistic understanding of the problem to be solved or what needs to improve.

> Action without an articulated outcome and plan will lead you everywhere and nowhere.

Action without an articulated outcome and plan will lead you everywhere and nowhere.

Return to why your organisation exists and its vision, then move to the next step.

FOCUS ON STRATEGY

Not having a vision of where you want to go is like walking along a road without knowing where you'll end up. At some point, you'll get tired of walking, forget why you started and sit down.

Our purpose in working with others is to understand what they want to achieve and the problems they need to solve while respecting their contribution to the vision.

Leaders come from a place of calm wisdom, balanced by humility to co-design what is needed to enhance performance, and can inspire intrinsic partnership for action.

People don't need telling how to do their job. At least initially, their existence in the organisation is proof that a recruitment process found them suitable to perform the necessary functions. If they are no longer fit for the role, look at the processes and systems that block them from delivering or moving on.

The EX team suffered from a lack of investment from their branch head. He knew there were problems but didn't prioritise time to listen before relaying

> Leaders come from a place of calm wisdom, balanced by humility to co-design what is needed to enhance performance, and can inspire intrinsic partnership for action.

expectations and openly telling others across the organisation that he didn't understand the value of the team and that he'd be happy to get rid of them.

The more I got to know the team and other teams in the branch, the more I understood that in the branch head's transition to senior executive, he'd unknowingly become a disconnected outsider. If the branch was playing rugby, he was always a play behind the rest of the team.

You're only as fast as your slowest teammate

In the few interactions I had with him, he admitted that things weren't running the way they should. I could feel his pain and see that he cared and genuinely wanted to turn things around. His major challenge was that he was under so much pressure to put out multiple fires and avoid a catastrophic failure that he couldn't create the structure and calm for a more preventative and sustainable improvement focus. The people in his inner circle weren't helping him either because, as the outer circle described, they were mini versions of him.

Operating in constant crisis wasn't helping him, and behind the scenes, people were seriously worried about his health. With overdue work and last-minute cancellations, he was always behind schedule. Time for self-care and time to attend to the people in his branch was virtually non-existent. People had given up trying to engage with him because it was clear that he didn't have any capacity. And when they were finally able to see him, he was so stressed and distracted that they didn't feel any benefit. Conversations were rushed, directions were given, and the churn continued.

The EX team was miserable and even stopped displaying the industry awards they had received. When I asked why, they said it was too depressing to see that their skills were recognised externally but not used or valued internally.

Having tried and failed to get traction on their behalf, I also didn't trust that anything would change under the existing senior executive. The most positive and lasting impact could be made by working directly with middle managers and the team.

Regardless of what has happened during operational lifecycles, if you've acknowledged past events or issues and worked with people to establish good relationships, it's likely you'll find active partners for change.

Although there is value in developing high-level strategies, roadmaps, and plans, these can often be produced in isolation and with limited access to teams who offer the greatest intelligence on what is needed for success.

Strategies can feel like a parachute someone has packed

> Strategies can feel like a parachute someone has packed for you, so you land safely after jumping from a plane. The expertise and care of the person who packed it better be massive because your existence depends on it.

for you, so you land safely after jumping from a plane. The expertise and care of the person who packed it better be massive because your existence depends on it.

The Group had a strategy, but it still required translation with clear business plans that flowed into the team and individual activities to achieve it. These plans had to be crafted on the understanding that they couldn't be all things to all people and do everything at once.

The EX team had become a dumping ground and needed to reset and manage expectations of themselves and others if they wanted to achieve anything aligned to the broader group strategy and enterprise-wide vision.

To deliver a realistic and achievable plan, they needed a practical and reflective approach to determine where to start and why.

> To bring strategy to life, give the HEART+SOUL of trust to hear people's perspectives of success and then facilitate partnerships to achieve it.

To bring strategy to life, give the HEART+SOUL of trust to hear people's perspectives of success and then facilitate partnerships to achieve it.

Moving beyond commonly taught managerial and leadership coaching processes, many 2020 studies found that a variety of techniques and activities should be used for reflection, problem-solving, and innovation to have significantly positive impacts.[99, 100, 101, 102, 103, 104]

Examples of creative coaching include being in different environments, coaching during activities, using stories, metaphors, symbols, and signs, and incorporating objects or media such as music and film to stimulate discussion.

In doing so, it's essential to understand what the intended outcomes will feel and look like for others and be clear on whether you're expecting long or short-term investment. This will also give you an indicator of the alternatives people may be open to.

Ask thought-provoking questions that demonstrate trust in people's ability to solve the problem. Support higher energy conversations and ideas that are solution-focused and enhance performance.

Be prepared to experiment and sit back a little to see what activities provide the best fit, add the most immediate value, and can be scaled further. This is far more powerful than pushing people to deliver an overwhelming, confusing, and desperate, everything-must-transform program.[105, 106]

We used a sneaky hot process in the EX team – like the uncool kids at school who become the most inspiring and attractive people at the reunion a few years later. Our goal was to quietly rebuild team members' skills and confidence, to get their light shining so brightly that people would be blinded by their awesomeness, and listen to apply the insights and improve organisational services more broadly.

If the organisation was committed to its strategy of shifting to a customer-centric culture, now was the time to adopt customer-centric thinking to improve the employee experience as well.

PRIORITISE AND DECIDE

*'The most urgent decisions are
rarely the most important ones.'*

– Dwight D. Eisenhower[107]

Made famous in Stephen Covey's book, *The 7 Habits of Highly Effective People*,[108] the Eisenhower Decision Matrix is more often known as the Urgent-Important Matrix. It consists of four categories to prioritise and decide on tasks:

1. **High value – urgent**

   This is about addressing needs for what might be considered a burning platform. You need to do these things now because if you don't, the consequences will be dire. Be warned, though, if people are always in this space, there is no room for innovation and growth.

2. **High value – not urgent**

   Tasks in this space are aligned with business strategy and plans, where action is clear, calm, and planned with a systems focus. If the organisation is running smoothly, this is where people's effort and energy should mostly be. This is the best area for people to learn, adapt and enhance services.

3. Low value – urgent

This is where smoke and spot fires occur because of poor decisions made earlier. Activities in this space could probably have been prevented with better understanding, planning and preparation. If this continues for extended periods, skilled and clever people will start looking for other opportunities because work here is frustrating.

4. Low value – not urgent

Is this still worth doing? If it doesn't fit with strategic and operational objectives and people can't provide evidence for why it is important or what happens if they stop doing it, perhaps it's time to eliminate this and focus on high-value opportunities and activities.

This approach is also something I learned in the military, we summed it up as the 5 Ps, which meant Prior Planning Prevents Poor Performance, and when used with a multi-disciplinary lens, it works.

Before you act, understand what the focus is and needs to be, now and for the future.

1. **Acknowledge the reality** that there are a finite number of resources available at any one point in time.
2. **Address crisis emotions and reactions** by connecting, if possible, in an environment that facilitates more considered return on investment thinking.
3. **Analyse the employee and customer experience** to ensure the problem has been adequately framed.

- Request access to people who can enhance perspective on what is or isn't needed holistically, and why at a deeper level.
- Use solution-focused questions.
- Partner with multi-disciplinary people to co-design cohesive solutions and approaches for implementation and continuous improvement.

4. **Adopt a risk planning, management, and mitigation approach** to decide what to focus on, why, when, and with whom.

- Know who is responsible for leading what and when.
- Obtain facts for evidence-based decision-making.
- Be clear regarding people's capability, scope, and responsibility.
- Understand the impact of change.
- Provide support that gives people the best chance of success.

5. **Accept** that circumstances can and will likely change, commit to reassessing the situation regularly and be flexible to re-prioritise as needed.

Know your purpose, what this means for others, and co-create

> Know your purpose, what this means for others, and co-create an actionable plan to provide genuine value. You'll need this before people commit to the work for achieving it.

an actionable plan to provide genuine value. You'll need this before people commit to the work for achieving it.

REFLECTION

- How would you perform with complete trust?
- How can you create optimal experiences for employees and customers?
- What needs to stop?
- What needs to continue?
- What needs to start?
- What are the consequences if things don't change?
- Who will help you identify, prepare for, and manage risks?

CHAPTER 10

COMMIT

We all have options. We can lay blame, justify, or accept responsibility and own what we can control. With ownership comes a sense of power, authority, and commitment to a cause.

Being committed is hiring a personal trainer, putting effort into every assigned workout, and following the eating plan consistently, even when you don't want to.

> Being committed is hiring a personal trainer, putting effort into every assigned workout, and following the eating plan consistently, even when you don't want to.

The EX team had the answers they needed to partner up and create a higher value proposition after connecting and clarifying together. More significantly, they were committed and had faith in themselves.

To stay the course through any significant change, people

need unwavering confidence in their value and ability to shift. Of equal importance is permission from individuals and teams to lead and provide support to build, advocate for, and grow their abilities.

When supporting others, particularly as a coach, manager, or executive, people need to know and feel that we're just as committed (and at times even more so) as they are.

Senior Executives needed to see that employee expertise was vital, facilitate partnerships with people across the organisation, leverage the team's new service offer, and support further development for larger scale benefits.

Given the years that had pulled the team down, it took six months to create an outwardly noticeable positive shift. We did so by applying everything in this book and focussing on what was meaningful, within their control, and achievable.

The larger organisational strategy to become customer-centric was not within the team's control but being clear on how they could enable and support gave them the confidence to chunk it down and build maturity over time.

What kept the team going was their desire and decision to provide holistic evidence-based recommendations, improvements, and support for others to inform enterprise-wide delivery. With discipline, consistency, and trust, they believed they could make a positive and lasting contribution.

When it comes to doing something you haven't done before or significantly changing the way you do things, you need to be committed for the change to occur. Your continued commitment is also required for improvements to be sustainable and mature over time.

Commitment requires decision, discipline, consistency, and trust, and this needs to become a natural way of being.

> Commitment requires decision, discipline, consistency, and trust, and this needs to become a natural way of being.

DECISION

Decisions lead to action. Broadly speaking, we make two types of decisions, either:

- Judgment decisions – where we aren't 100 per cent certain of the outcome because it's new, and we need to rely more on data analysis, interpretation, and experimentation.
- Definite decisions – where there is a right and wrong answer, for example, mathematical problems.[109]

Life would be much less complicated if we worked off right or wrong, but our world has so much variability that we would be mad to think and act in terms of absolutes. We would probably also become disinterested.

Being experimental and flexible with the unknown isn't always a natural thing to do, particularly if we need to make hard decisions and act.

Regardless of the type of decision to be made, if we're operating with uncertainty and changing conditions, it's also worth checking that we, and those around us, aren't falling into decision inertia or holding onto a decision that no longer serves the desired outcome.

Decision inertia is not about avoiding or being unable to decide; it's where we choose not to act on the decision. This occurs out of fear or concern due to the level of uncertainty and significant (often irreversible) consequences if the decision is wrong.[110]

Alternatively, people can hold too tightly to the initial decision, despite new evidence and better choices, which suggest that an alternative focus or direction is needed.

Interestingly, research has shown that those who are emotionally resilient to negative consequences and action-oriented are more prone to this, particularly if we made the decision.[111]

> We need to make decisions and act based on what we know now, who we have, and the resources available to support the outcome.

We need to make decisions and act based on what we know now, who we have, and the resources available to support the outcome.

To mitigate decision inertia and increase the likelihood of success, ensure that decisions are:

- Evidence-based
- Made from critical thinking

- In consideration of impacts across people, process, and technology
- Focussed on the outcome, not the people making the decisions
- Collaborative, to leverage the perspectives and strengths of multiple disciplines
- Adaptive, in that they are reviewed, open for dissent, and adjusted as needed.[112, 113, 114]

DISCIPLINE

Once decisions are made, the ability to stay the course and be adaptable when circumstances shift will determine success or failure. Discipline is commonly defined as the practice of obeying a set of rules or code of behaviour, or a branch of knowledge or study.[115, 116]

For trust, it's useful to think of discipline as a combination of rules, behaviour, and knowledge. We're seeking to honour our own codes, respect those of others, and be committed to learning and growth for a higher purpose.

Being disciplined at work can be

> For trust, it's useful to think of discipline as a combination of rules, behaviour, and knowledge. We're seeking to honour our own codes, respect those of others, and be committed to learning and growth for a higher purpose.

challenging and even unrealistic. Uncertainty is unavoidable, so we're frequently under stress because we do not and cannot control everything.

While we need to accept and adapt to uncertainty, we can examine stress as either healthy or harmful and then focus our efforts more productively – particularly if we're seeking improvements.

Not everything is worthy of sustained effort, and numerous studies have examined the relationship between workplace stress and innovation. When attaining work goals, we can broadly categorise three main classes of stress or demand on employees.

Challenge stressors are healthy where there is a balance between the task and our ability to perform. Here we develop mastery and grow.

Hindrance stressors are unhelpful; the work is too hard or boring, and motivation and performance are reduced.

Threat demands need to be addressed and removed as a matter of urgency; these involve interpersonal and role conflicts, such as bullying and injustice.[117, 118]

Healthy stress that supports adaptation is worth being disciplined for, and this is about chasing and achieving flow.

Flow is when you lose track of time because you're completely engaged and enjoying what you're doing. It happens when working on meaningful tasks, where we have a level of autonomy and control, and our skills match the task at hand, while we're still challenged and feel a sense of progress.

You could call it challenging fun. Research has also shown that being in flow significantly enhances motivation, creativity, problem-solving, decision-making, and overall performance.[119, 120, 121]

> Discipline comes from chasing and doing what lights you up. Find ways to enable and support flow among teams more broadly, and awesome results will follow.

Discipline comes from chasing and doing what lights you up. Find ways to enable and support flow among teams more broadly, and awesome results will follow.

Consistency

With our thoughts, feelings, and energy levels on a sliding scale of experience, there will be times when motivation is lacking. That's why I mentioned the usefulness of being disciplined by chasing flow.

Consistency is about showing up even when you don't want to.

Once the initial excitement of building something new is over, it will likely take more time and effort than expected or desired if it's something of real value and importance. This is particularly the case if you're keeping the lights on and delivering existing services while innovating and developing others.

It's a little like maintaining a family household, working, and embarking on a new fitness and healthy lifestyle regime. The habits that we've established over time will work for or against us, and changing these can be tough.

CEOS Theory offers a common perspective on behaviour that is hard to maintain. The acronym stands for Context, Executive, and Operational Systems and focuses on why some changes can be difficult to sustain, even with compelling evidence that our behaviour needs to shift. For example, quitting harmful habits like smoking and overcoming other addictions to live healthier lifestyles, or being more value-driven, resourceful, and cost-effective at work.

The CEOS theory suggests that behaviour change can be hard because we're working off two overarching systems that control our behaviour – the executive system, and the operational system – alongside our environment and physical resources.

Our executive system (ES) uses conscious thought and cognitive control for more deliberate and pro-active pursuits, for example, reasoning, problem-solving and planning. Our operational system (OS) uses unconscious functions that oversee feelings and motor control, for example, what we consider to be pleasure and pain, our vocal and physical expressions of emotion, and routine tasks such as getting dressed and brushing our teeth.

Mostly the ES and OS work together, but when we're trying to break unhelpful behaviours or habits and establish new behaviours that better serve our goals and aspirations, these systems compete against each other. It's this conflict that creates a bucket load of negativity.[122]

Contextually at a team and organisational level, if you're trying to implement change, you're looking to override multiple conscious and unconscious systems that keep people locked into old ways of working. We can all decide that the change will be good, but unconscious systems require a significant amount of awareness, focus and sustained effort for the change to occur and be embedded.

An over-reliance on individuals' strengths can create useless single points of fail. Collective and consistent efforts of everyone, are what produce sustainable, long-term results for organisations and those they serve.

In his book, *Atomic Habits*, James Clear highlights the importance of consistency and outlines ways to break old behaviours and establish better ones. *Atomic Habits* really helped me prepare for my first bodybuilding competition. I had a brilliant coach in Justin Burton, numerous accountability partners cheering from the sidelines, and for the most part, I had the desire, but it was the consistency of effort when I wanted to give up that produced the result.

> An over-reliance on individuals' strengths can create useless single points of fail. Collective and consistent efforts of everyone, are what produce sustainable, long-term results for organisations and those they serve.

In addition to what we've described under Commit and Clarify, the best way to achieve consistency is to:

- Pair new ways of working with established practices you want to keep
- Make the new way of working intuitively easier
- Avoid old practices by removing the ability to keep doing them, or make it considerably harder than adopting new ones
- Accept that occasional setbacks and plateaus are part of the process
- Acknowledge, own and celebrate small wins
- Partner with people who will check-in, hold you accountable and be supportive.[123, 124]

> It's vital to chunk effort down to what is achievable, with who and what you have now. So too is finding people who provide you with HEART+SOUL.

It's vital to chunk effort down to what is achievable, with who and what you have now. So too is finding people who provide you with HEART+SOUL.

It's also why applying what we've covered in this book and working with others to co-design solutions and the approaches for implementing them is non-negotiable.

Trust

By now, you either have this, or you don't.

Not surprisingly, proximity also matters, and research has demonstrated that the emotional connection people have with their colleagues and direct managers has a greater impact on their commitment to the organisation and its outcomes than their feelings about the organisation itself.[125, 126]

Culture is influenced by the way we work together.[127] Relationships founded on trust are strong, and the more of these you have across all levels and areas of the organisation, the greater the benefits.

Without trust, people will sit back and watch to see if you fail before they get on board. Without their help and support, chances are this will become a self-fulfilling prophecy.

With trust, you have equal partners prepared to work to get the outcome regardless of whether anyone is watching because they have full faith that the effort will be worth it. Furthermore, high-trust teams are more transparent and openly discuss when things don't feel right or aren't going to plan. They rely on each other and seek assistance to work better as

Blind commitment serves no one, so if you're all faltering, perhaps it's time to check whether the approach and support need to be adapted or changed.

individuals and as a team – they're also more committed to staying for future work.[128]

Sure, we all have times when our belief waivers, and we need reminders of why we're doing things differently or working a little harder, but the benefit of working in partnership means that we're all in it together. When one of us falters, the other lifts so we get there as one team.

Blind commitment serves no one, so if you're all faltering, perhaps it's time to check whether the approach and support need to be adapted or changed.

HONOUR THOSE WHO SERVE

Honour everyone you meet for the experience that you only get to see the surface of. As individuals, we have rich histories, stories, and ways of being that have brought us to where we are today.

> Working together brings opportunities to unlock and learn from multiple intelligences and perspectives that we could never gain on our own in a million lifetimes.

Working together brings opportunities to unlock and learn from multiple intelligences and perspectives that we could never gain on our own in a million lifetimes.

When it comes to leadership, we each lead and serve in some way, whether at work, for ourselves, our family, and friends.

Find and follow the people who others trust because they are already honoured as leaders among their community. They have done the hard work to understand the culture and the people they work with at a deep level.

If you don't have street cred, leverage off someone who does because they will be your greatest adversary or strongest ally – partner with them for the greater good. Aligning yourself with internally trusted authorities offers greater freedom to move and significantly enhances your understanding of how you can deliver enduring value.

Earning the trust of respected informal leaders often provides broader, far-reaching opportunities for greater value and builds a legacy.

UNLOCK THE MAGIC IN OTHERS

When we begin working together, my mission is to leave people better. I love doing myself out of a job, knowing that the people I work with are capable and confident to continue and grow without me.

A member of the EX team likened me to Mary Poppins, who floats in, works some magic, and then floats off to help someone else. The title still brings a smile to my face, and it's probably a funnier way of describing what lights me up.

Truth be told, I don't work the magic; it's that I've learned how to unlock it in others.

The magic comes from feeling, hearing, seeing, and sensing

between the gaps of what is communicated and shown, then working with people through the mud, sweat and tears.

To wrap up our story, the collective wisdom of multiple individuals and organisations represented as the EX team has been developed and accepted as an employee and customer experience (CX) strategy and quality framework for Whole of Australian Government Shared Services.[129]

This employee developed and owned CX approach is the first to directly support operational alignment with the intent of the Australian Digital Service Platform Strategy to 'build trust and confidence',[130] while supporting the Australian Government's intent to become 'a trusted APS'.[131]

That's a long and technical way of saying that with trust, people can exceed all expectations as they honour their code, play their best, and achieve amazing things. And if their own organisations don't recognise and make the most of their internal value, they'll always have opportunities to shine elsewhere.

HEART+SOUL and the 3Cs of Connect, Clarify, and Commit can be hard work, but it's the challenges and quirks of life that make things interesting, allow us to grow, and inspire us to be better than we are today.

In a world of uncertainty, we need to trust ourselves and each other.

In a world of uncertainty, we need to trust ourselves and each other.

214

BRINGING IT TOGETHER

We've covered a lot of ground in this book, and I promised to deliver a succinct and practical way to build what you've learned into something useful to take away and make your own.

So, here is a handy chart of Now, Next, and Later things you might like to consider before exploring your specifics.

ENGAGE	NOW	NEXT	LATER
HEART+ SOUL	Be passionate about being in service Remember that it's not about you	Determine if this a long or short game Be inclusive and adaptable	Be comfortable with your advice being theirs
CONNECT	Be fully present and listen Use non-verbal cues and create safety for people to share the truth	Seek to understand the experience Find the feeling, and search for meaning	Show and accept humanity Reflect on interactions and the importance of partnership with them
CLARIFY	Embrace that you don't know everything Identify the strategic and operational opportunities, risks, and issues Use solution-focused questions to co-create a meaningful vision and realistic plan for success	Know the consequences for action or in-action Adopt credible curiosity for other people's ideas Co-design quality and assurance requirements, accountabilities, and support systems	Prioritise effort using a systems-thinking and evidence-based approach Obtain and do what is needed for achievable and scalable continuous improvement
COMMIT	Invite and support ownership for outcomes Create confidence by 'being' and 'doing'	Prepare to give more by lifting others higher	Give the team the glory

Table 5: Implementing trust: now, next and later

OVER TO YOU

With HEART+SOUL, there is a quiet confidence that if your current organisation doesn't value you, then you can always take your thinking and skills to organisations, teams and individuals that do.

Individually and collectively, people can and will dig deep during multiple highs and lows. Self-leadership is enhanced when we offer people ownership for what they can control. There are always ways to influence more broadly by modelling what we would like from others.

> Together we are stronger and more capable than we imagine on our own. Trust is the foundation of healthy organisations with connected, clear, and committed people.

Together we are stronger and more capable than we imagine on our own. Trust is the foundation of healthy organisations with connected, clear, and committed people.

How will you lead with HEART+SOUL?

ACKNOWLEDGMENTS

Thank you for allowing me to share my first book with you. I value your time, reflection and welcome an understanding of your thoughts along the way.

This has been a very personal journey. It would not have been possible without the trust and honour of working with the individuals, teams, and organisations whose stories I've shared. I deeply respect and continue to be inspired by people I connect with personally and professionally.

Thank you to the talented and dedicated researchers and authors who enable and support evidence-based practice.

The most significant contributor to my brain has been The Oxford Review. David Wilkinson and his team work incredibly hard to provide brilliantly curated papers and reports in easy to consume, highly practical formats. The research and insights you share with members and the way you do so are invaluable.

With absolute gratitude, Peter Cook, Matt Church, Lisa O'Neill, Col Fink, Linda Hutchings, extended faculty members, and friends of Thought Leaders Business School, connecting with you is my BEST DECISION EVER!

Thank you, Jenny Magee, for your time and care in editing this book. It was wonderful to trust you through the process.

To my beautiful daughter Hayley, I continue to be amazed by your talents and am so grateful for your design of this book's cover.

To my brothers, sisters, work husbands and wives, you have listened to so many of my fears, ramblings, and rants over the years, getting me through to clarity and calm. You know who you are, and I love you like crazy!

For Anthony, Hayley, Hayden, Mum and Dad. It is for you, and through your love, strength, wisdom, patience, and guidance that I am who I am today, and who I will be tomorrow. I love you the most, to infinity and beyond.

Support others

In purchasing this book, you have supported others. Fifty per cent of the book proceeds are donated to the Foundation for Indigenous Sustainable Health (FISH).

FISH is an organisation that seeks to bring healing to the spirit, heart, mind, body, and land to help create healthy people and communities.

The organisation also aims to provide opportunities for Aboriginal and Torres Strait Islander people to share their wisdom and insights to the broader community to teach people how to connect and care for each other and for country, while

ACKNOWLEDGMENTS

closing the gap and breaking generational cycles of poverty, trauma, and engagement with the justice system.

For more information, go to www.fish.asn.au

ABOUT THE AUTHOR

Melanie Marshall is an evidence-based coach and trust strategist who offers a blend of thinking and methodologies. She mixes practical experience with solid evidence, ensuring her deep knowledge is up to date with the latest research.

As a bridge between organisational strategy and delivery, Melanie partners with executives, leaders, and operational areas to improve the way they do things – for employees, customers, and the community. Her focus is on unlocking the magic of individuals and teams by co-creating trust so people can sustainably deliver services they're proud of.

For more than 25 years, Melanie has worked with leaders and teams at all levels, in private industry, federal and state government, local council, and the Australian military.

With an eclectic career as a military veteran, personal trainer, public servant, service delivery executive, and leadership advisor, the common thread is Melanie's passion for enabling and supporting people to be the best version of themselves. It sounds sentimental, but it's true.

She is renowned for her ability to listen and identify what matters most, clearing noise and drama and keeping things real.

TRUST

As an energetic presenter, Melanie is magnetically attracted to a whiteboard and wearing heels that are sometimes hard to walk in.

Melanie and her family have recently settled in Brisbane, and when not coaching or delivering programs, Melanie mostly enjoys the gym but loves ice cream and time with the kids more.

For more information about Melanie's programs, visit melaniemarshall.com.au

Connect via LinkedIn linkedin.com/in/melanie-marshall-4a487b68

Email melanie@melaniemarshall.com.au

REFERENCES

1. Oxford. (2017). *Australian Pocket Oxford Dictionary* (7th Edition), Oxford University Press Australia

2. Wilkinson. D.J. (2019). When Transformational Leadership Meets Cynicism; Oxford Review Special Report. *The Oxford Review.* www.oxford-review.com

3. Wilkinson. D.J. (2019). When Transformational Leadership Meets Cynicism; Oxford Review Special Report. *The Oxford Review.* www.oxford-review.com

4. Australian Government Department of the Prime Minister and Cabinet. (2019). *Our Public Service, Our Future. Independent Review of the Australian Public Service.* Sourced from https://pmc.gov.au/sites/default/files/publications/independent-review-aps.pdf

5. Australian Government Department of the Prime Minister and Cabinet. (2019). *Our Public Service, Our Future. Independent Review of the Australian Public Service.* Sourced from https://pmc.gov.au/sites/default/files/publications/independent-review-aps.pdf

6. Australian Government. (2019). *Independent review of the Australian Public Service.* Sourced from https://www.apsreview.gov.au/

7. Australian Government Department of the Prime Minister and Cabinet. (2019). *Our Public Service, Our Future. Independent Review of the Australian Public Service.* Sourced from https://pmc.gov.au/sites/default/files/publications/independent-review-aps.pdf

8. Khan, W. A. (1990). Psychological Conditions of Personal Engagement and Disengagement at Work. *Academy of Management Journal.* 33 (4), 692-724.

9. Khan, W. A. (1990). Psychological Conditions of Personal Engagement and Disengagement at Work. *Academy of Management Journal.* 33 (4), 692-724.

10. Lee, Y., Shin, H. Y., Park, J., Kim, W., & Cho, D. (2017). An integrative literature review on employee engagement in the field of human resource

development: exploring where we are and where we should go. *Asia Pacific Education Review*, 18(4), 541-557.

11. Wilkinson. D.J. (2019). High-Performance Teams: What the research says; Oxford Review Special Report. *The Oxford Review*. www.oxford-review.com

12. Wilkinson. D.J. (2019). High-Performance Teams: What the research says; Oxford Review Special Report. *The Oxford Review*. www.oxford-review.com

13. Wilkinson. D.J. (2020). How Businesses Pivot Successfully: What the research says; Oxford Review Special Report. *The Oxford Review*. www.oxford-review.com

14. Scammell. J. (2020). *Service Mindset: 6 mindsets to lead a high-performing service team*. Melbourne: Major Street Publishing.

15. Robertson, F. (2020). *Rules of Belonging: Change your organisational culture, delight your people and turbo-charge your results*. Melbourne: Major Street Publishing.

16. McHale, S. (2020). *The Insider's Guide to Culture Change: Creating a Workplace That Delivers, Grows, and Adapts*. Nashville, US: Harper Collins.

17. Kuntz, J., & Dehlin, E. (2019). Friend and foe? Self-deception in organisations. *Journal of Management Development*, 38(2), 130-140.

18. Hendrikz, K., & Engelbrecht, A. S. (2019). The principled leadership scale: An integration of value-based leadership. *SA Journal of Industrial Psychology*, 45, 1-10.

19. Zak. P. J. (2017). The Neuroscience of Trust. *Harvard Business Review*, January-February 2017 issue (pp.84-90). Sourced from https://hbr.org/2017/01/the-neuroscience-of-trust.

20. Preston, N., (July 19, 2020). *7 Signs of Gaslighting at the Workplace*. https://www.psychologytoday.com/au/blog/communication-success/202007/7-signs-gaslighting-the-workplace

21. DiBenigno, J. (2018). Rapid Relationality: How Peripheral Experts Build a Foundation for Influence with Line Managers. *Administrative Science Quarterly*. January 2019, DOI: 10.1177/0001839219827006.

22. Bird, L., Gretton, M., Cockerell, R., & Heathcote, A. (2019). The cognitive load of narrative lies. *Applied Cognitive Psychology*, 33(5), 936-942.

23. La Tona, G., Terranova, M. C., Vernuccio, F., Re, G. L., Salerno, S., Zerbo, S.,

& Argo, A. (2020). Lie Detection: fMRI. *Radiology in Forensic Medicine*, Chapter 18, 197- 202. Springer, Cham.

24. Yin, L., & Weber, B. (2019). I lie, why don't you: Neural mechanisms of individual differences in self-serving lying. *Human Brain Mapping*, 40(4), 1101-1113. doi: 10.1002/hbm.24432. Epub 2018 Oct 24. PMID: 30353970; PMCID: PMC6865395.

25. Creasey, T. *The Costs and Risks of Poorly Managed Change*. https://blog.prosci.com/the-costs-risks-of-poorly-managed-change

26. McDougall, M., Ronkainen, N., Richardson, D., Littlewood, M., & Nesti, M. (2019). Three team and organisational culture myths and their consequences for sport psychology research and practice. *International Review of Sport and Exercise Psychology*, 13, 1-16.

27. Miller, V. D., Johnson, J. R., & Grau, J. (1994). Antecedents to willingness to participate in a planned organizational change. *Journal of Applied Communication Research,* 22, 59–80.

28. Wanberg, C. R., & Banas, J. T. (2000). Predictors and outcomes of openness to changes in a reorganizing workplace. *Journal of Applied Psychology*, 85, 132–142.

29. Armenakis, A., & Bedeian, A. G. (1999). Organizational change: A review of theory and research in the 1990s. *Journal of Management*, 25, 293–315.

30. Devos, G., Buelens, M., & Bouckenooghe, D. (2007). Contribution of content, context, and process to understanding openness to organizational change: Two experimental simulation studies. *The Journal of Social Psychology*, 147(6), 607-630.

31. Goleman, D. (2000). *Working with Emotional Intelligence*. London: Bantam Press.

32. Doz, Y. (2020). Fostering strategic agility: How individual executives and human resource practices contribute. *Human Resource Management Review*, 30(1), 100693.

33. Brisbane City Council. (2020). *Community Garden Guide*. Sourced from https://www.brisbane.qld.gov.au/clean-and-green/green-home-and-community/community-groups/community-gardens-and-city-farms/community-garden-guide

34. Brisbane City Council. (2020). *Community Garden Guide*. Sourced from https://www.brisbane.qld.gov.au/clean-and-green/green-home-and-

community/community-groups/community-gardens-and-city-farms/
community-garden-guide

35. Zenger, J. & Folkman, J. (February 05, 2019). The 3 Elements of Trust. *Harvard Business Review*. Sourced from https://hbr.org/2019/02/the-3-elements-of-trust

36. Zenger, J. & Folkman, J. (February 05, 2019). The 3 Elements of Trust. *Harvard Business Review*. Sourced from https://hbr.org/2019/02/the-3-elements-of-trust

37. Doz, Y. (2020). Fostering strategic agility: How individual executives and human resource practices contribute. *Human Resource Management Review*, 30(1), 100693.

38. Wilkinson. D.J. (2020). How Businesses Pivot Successfully: What the research says; Oxford Review Special Report. *The Oxford Review*. www.oxford-review.com

39. Dreeke, R. & Stauth, C. (2017). *The Code of Trust – An American counterintelligence expert's five rules to lead and succeed*. New York: St. Martin's Press.

40. Routh, Z. (2016). *Composure: How centred leaders make the biggest impact*. Australia: Inner Compass.

41. Graßmann, C., Schölmerich, F., & Schermuly, C. C. (2020). The relationship between working alliance and client outcomes in coaching: A meta-analysis. *Human Relations*, 73(1), 35-58.

42. Newman, M. (2014). *Emotional Capitalists: The Ultimate Guide to Developing Emotional Intelligence for Leaders*. Milton, Qld: John Wiley & Sons Australia.

43. Orange Sky Australia. https://orangesky.org.au/

44. Roche Martin. (2016) *Emotional Capital Report*. Sourced from https://www.rochemartin.com/tools/emotional-capital-report-ecr/

45. Reichheld, F. & Markey, R. (2011). *The Ultimate Question 2.0: How Net Promoter Companies Thrive in a Customer-Driven World*. Boston, USA: Harvard Business Review Press.

46. NICE Satmetrix. *What is Net Promoter?* Sourced from https://www.netpromoter.com/know/

47. Schlegel, K., Palese. T., Schmid Mast, M., Rammsayer,T. H., Hall, J. A., & Murphy, N. A. (2019). A meta-analysis of the relationship between

emotion recognition ability and intelligence, *Cognition and Emotion*, DOI: 10.1080/02699931.2019.1632801.

48. Schlegel, K., Palese. T., Schmid Mast, M., Rammsayer,T. H., Hall, J. A., & Murphy, N. A. (2019). A meta-analysis of the relationship between emotion recognition ability and intelligence, *Cognition and Emotion*, DOI: 10.1080/02699931.2019.1632801.

49. McLeod, S. (February 05, 2018). *Cognitive Dissonance*. https://www.simplypsychology.org/cognitive-dissonance.html

50. Appelbaum, N. P., Lockeman, K. S., Orr, S., Huff, T. A., Hogan, C. J., Queen, B. A., & Dow, A. W. (2020). Perceived influence of power distance, psychological safety, and team cohesion on team effectiveness. *Journal of Interprofessional Care*, 34(1), 20-26.

51. Yunkaporta, T. (2019). *Sand Talk: how indigenous thinking can save the world*. Melbourne: Text Publishing.

52. Grant, A. M. (2017). Solution-focused cognitive–behavioral coaching for sustainable high performance and circumventing stress, fatigue, and burnout. *Consulting Psychology Journal*: Practice and Research, 69(2), 98.

53. http://www.greatthoughtstreasury.com/author/joseph-sanial-dubay

54. Dictionary. (2021) sincerity. Vocabulary.com [online]. Available at https://www.vocabulary.com/dictionary/sincerity

55. emotional labour. *Oxford Reference*. Retrieved 2 Mar. 2021, from. https://www.oxfordreference.com/view/10.1093/oi/authority.20110803095749956

56. Hochschild, A. R. (2012). *The Managed Heart: Commercialization of Human Feeling*. Berkeley: University of California Press.

57. Kaur, H., & Kaur, S. (2019). Emotional Labour-An Empirical Analysis of Its Correlation with Well Being. *OPUS: HR Journal*, 10(1), 122.

58. Levine. E. E., Roberts. A. R., & Cohen. T. R. (2020). Difficult Conversations: Navigating the tension between honesty and benevolence. *Current Opinion in Psychology*. 31. 10.1016/j.copsyc.2019.07.034.

59. Stone, D., Patton, B., & Heen, S. (2010). *Difficult Conversations: How to discuss what matters most*. New York: Penguin.

60. Saha, S. (2020). Driving Performance Through Appreciative Inquiry: Role of Pygmalion Effect in Academics and Industry. In *Appreciative Inquiry Approaches to Organizational Transformation* (pp. 1-18). IGI Global.

61. Tocino-Smith, J. (September 30, 2020). *How to Apply Appreciative Inquiry: A Visual Guide*. https://positivepsychology.com/appreciative-inquiry-process/

62. Orr, T., & Cleveland-Innes. M. (2015). Appreciative leadership: Supporting education innovation. *International Review of Research in Open and Distributed Learning*, 16(4), 235-240.

63. Sandu, A., & Damian, S. (2012). Applying appreciative inquiry principles in the restorative justice field, *Postmodern Openings*, 2012, Volume 3, Issue 2, June, 37-52.

64. Farahnak, L. R., Ehrhart, M. G., Torres, E. M., & Aarons, G. A. (2020). The influence of transformational leadership and leader attitudes on subordinate attitudes and implementation success. *Journal of Leadership & Organizational Studies*, 27(1), 98-111.

65. Wilkinson. D.J. (2019). When transformational leadership meets cynicism; Oxford Review Special Report. *The Oxford Review*. www.oxford-review.com

66. Wilkinson. D.J. (2019). When transformational leadership meets cynicism; Oxford Review Special Report. *The Oxford Review*. www.oxford-review.com

67. Wilkinson. D.J. (2019). When transformational leadership meets cynicism; Oxford Review Special Report. *The Oxford Review*. www.oxford-review.com

68. Vic Health. (March 18, 2020). *Bright Futures Challenge projects*. Sourced from https://www.vichealth.vic.gov.au/programs-and-projects/bright-futures-projects

69. Senova, M. (2020). *This human: How to be the person designing for other people*. BIS Publishers.

70. Foundation for Indigenous Sustainable Health. https://fish.asn.au/

71. Lifeline Australia. *Annual Report 2018-2019*. Sourced from https://www.lifeline.org.au/static/uploads/files/web-lifeline-annual-r-2018-19-wfgeyleavrdw.pdf

72. Foundation for Indigenous Sustainable Health. https://fish.asn.au/

73. Farahnak, L. R., Ehrhart, M. G., Torres, E. M., & Aarons, G. A. (2020). The influence of transformational leadership and leader attitudes on subordinate attitudes and implementation success. *Journal of Leadership & Organizational Studies*, 27(1), 98-111.

ENDNOTES

74. Wilkinson. D.J. (2019) When transformational leadership meets cynicism; Oxford Review Special Report. *The Oxford Review.* www.oxford-review.com

75. Maister, D. H., Galford, R., & Green, C. (2001). *The Trusted Advisor.* New York: Simon & Schuster.

76. Lifeline Australia. *Annual Report 2018-2019.* Sourced from https://www.lifeline.org.au/static/uploads/files/web-lifeline-annual-r-2018-19-wfgeyleavrdw.pdf
    Brown, S.W., & Grant, A. M. (2010). From GROW to GROUP: Theoretical issues and a practical model for group coaching in organisations. *Coaching: An International Journey of Theory, Research and Practice,* 3, 30-45.
    Maister, D. H., Galford, R., & Green, C. (2001). *The Trusted Advisor.* New York: Simon & Schuster.
    Bushe, G.R. (2011). Appreciative inquiry: Theory and critique. In Boje, D., Burnes, B. & Hassard, J. (eds.) *The Routledge Companion To Organizational Change* (pp. 87103). Oxford, UK: Routledge.

77. Fraser, A. (2020). *Strive: Embracing the Gift of Struggle.* Milton, Qld: John Wiley & Sons Australia

78. Kübler-Ross, E., & Kessler, D. (2005). *On Grief and Grieving: Finding the meaning of grief through the five stages of loss.* Scribner (e-book).

79. Cialdini, R. B. (2016). *Pre-Suasion: A Revolutionary Way to Influence and Persuade.* New York: Simon & Schuster.

80. Christou, P., Avloniti, A., & Farmaki, A. (2019). Guests' perceptions of emotionally expressive and non-expressive service providers within the hospitality context. *International Journal of Hospitality Management,* 76, 152-162.

81. Yan, Z. (2018). How to Promote Employee Voice Behavior: Analysis Based on Leadership Style Perspective. *Journal of Research in Business, Economics and Management,* 10(1), 1814-1823.

82. Donaldson, M. (2013). *The Crossroad – A story of life, death and the SAS.* Macmillan.

83. Transitional Support. *Burnout Vs Compassion Fatigue.* Sourced from http://transitionalsupport.com.au/transitional-phase/compassion-fatigue-trauma/

84. *Professional Quality of Life Measure.* https://proqol.org/CS_and_CF.html

85. Khan, W. A. (1990). Psychological Conditions of Personal Engagement and Disengagement at Work. *Academy of Management Journal*. 33 (4): 692-724.

86. Goffee, R., & Jones, G. R. (2006). *Why Should Anyone Be Led by You? What It Takes to Be an Authentic Leader*. Emerald Group Publishing Limited.

87. Seligman, M. E. P. (2002). *Authentic Happiness: Using the new positive psychology to realize your potential for lasting fulfillment*. New York: Free Press.

88. Ackerman, C.E. *Learned Helplessness: Seligman's Theory of Depression (+Cure)*. Sourced from https://positivepsychology.com/learned-helplessness-seligman-theory-depression-cure/

89. Mapalala, M. J., West, G. R. B., & Winston, B. (2018). Examining the relationship between entrepreneurial orientation and organizational performance: The moderating role of organizational learning. *International Leadership Journal*, 10(3), 40-63.

90. Chisnall, G. (2020). *Trust in crisis: How to be trusted in the face of uncertainty*. Sourced from https://leftofboom.com.au

91. Chisnall, G. https://leftofboom.com.au/

92. Chisnall, G. (2020). *Trust in crisis: How to be trusted in the face of uncertainty*. Sourced from https://leftofboom.com.au

93. Wilkinson. D.J. (2020). Organisational Health – What the research says; Oxford Review Special Report. *The Oxford Review*. www.oxford-review.com

94. Lowe, D., & Yearworth, M. (2017). Ensuring continued enterprise resilience: developing a method for monitoring health. In *2016 Conference on systems engineering research*. Sourced from https://core.ac.uk

95. Thought Leaders Business School. www.thoughtleaders.com.au/business-school

96. Pignata, S., Boyd, C. M., Winefield, A. H., & Provis, C. (2017). Interventions: Employees' Perceptions of What Reduces Stress. *BioMed Research International*.

97. DiBenigno, J. (2018). Rapid Relationality: How Peripheral Experts Build a Foundation for Influence with Line Managers. *Administrative Science Quarterly*, 0001839219827006.

98. Kim, D. H. (1999). *Introduction to Systems Thinking*. Sourced from https://thesystemsthinker.com

99. Bacouël, C. (2020). Coaching, Agility and Sustainable Leadership. In *Sustainable Innovation: Trends in Marketing and Management* (pp. 71-79). Cham, Switzerland: Palgrave Pivot.

100. Lee, A., Legood, A., Hughes, D., Tian, A. W., Newman, A., & Knight, C. (2020). Leadership, creativity, and innovation: a meta-analytic review. *European Journal of Work and Organizational Psychology*, 29(1), 1-35.

101. Maisel, E. (Ed.). (2020). *The Creativity Workbook for Coaches and Creatives: 50+ Inspiring Exercises from Creativity Coaches Worldwide*. New York: Routledge.

102. Mikkelsen, T. (2020). *Coaching the Creative Impulse: Psychological Dynamics and Professional Creativity*. New York: Routledge.

103. Park, H. J., & Oh, S. J. (2020). The Effect of Managerial Coaching Behavior on Employees' Creativity in IT field: Focused on the Moderating Effect of Creative Self-efficacy and the Mediating Effect of Unlearning. *The Journal of the Korea Contents Association*, 20(3), 400-423.

104. Pan, W., Sun, L. Y., & Lam, L. W. (2020). Employee–organization exchange and employee creativity: A motivational perspective. *The International Journal of Human Resource Management*, 31(3), 385-407.

105. Cowan, J. (2017). Linking Reflective Activities for Self-managed Development of Higher-level Abilities. *Journal of Perspectives in Applied Academic Practice*, 5, 67-74.

106. Grant, A. M. (2017). Solution-focused cognitive–behavioral coaching for sustainable high performance and circumventing stress, fatigue, and burnout. *Consulting Psychology Journal: Practice and Research*, 69(2), 98.

107. Dwight D. Eisenhower. (2021, March, 02). In *Wikipedia*. https://en.wikipedia.org/wiki/Dwight_D._Eisenhower

108. Covey, S. R. (2013). *The 7 Habits of Highly Effective People* (25th Edition). New York: Simon & Schuster.

109. Wilkinson, D. (2019). Group decision-making. What the latest research says; Oxford Review Special Report. *The Oxford Review*. www.oxford-review.com

110. Power, N., Alison, L, Ralph, J. (2013). Decision inertia: Defining its meaning and dichotomising its context as a latent and emergent variable.

International Conference on Naturalistic Decision Making 2013, Marseille, France.

111. Jung, D., Erdfelder, Edgar, Broder, A., & Dorner, V. (2019). Differentiating motivational and cognitive explanations for decision inertia. *Journal of Economic Psychology*, 72, 30-44.

112. Tindale, R. S., & Winget, J. R. (2019). Group decision-making. In *Oxford Research Encyclopedia of Psychology*.[online].Sourced from https://oxfordre.com/psychology

113. Uhl-Bien, M., & Arena, M. (2018). Leadership for organizational adaptability: A theoretical synthesis and integrative framework. *The Leadership Quarterly*.

114. Wilkinson, D. (2019). Group decision-making. What the latest research says; Oxford Review Special Report. *The Oxford Review*. www.oxford-review.com

115. Dictionary. (2021). discipline. *Cambridge English Dictionary* [online]. Available at https://dictionary.cambridge.org/dictionary/english/discipline

116. Dictionary. (2021). discipline. *Oxford Learner's Dictionary* [online]. Available at https://www.oxfordlearnersdictionaries.com/definition/english/discipline_1

117. Montani, F., Vandenberghe, C., Khedhaouria, A., & Courcy, F. (2020). Examining the inverted U-shaped relationship between workload and innovative work behavior: The role of work engagement and mindfulness. *Human Relations*, 73(1), 59-93.

118. Pignata, S., Boyd, C. M., Winefield, A. H., & Provis, C. (2017). Interventions: Employees' Perceptions of What Reduces Stress. *BioMed Research International*.

119. Bakker, A. B., & van Woerkom, M. (2017). Flow at work: A self-determination perspective. *Occupational Health Science*, 1-19.

120. Liu, M., Huang, Y., & Zhang, D. (2017) Gamification's impact on manufacturing: Enhancing job motivation, satisfaction and operational performance with smartphone-based gamified job design. *Human Factors and Ergonomics in Manufacturing & Service Industries*, 28(2), 38-51.

121. Fraser, A. (2020). *Strive: Embracing the gift of struggle*. Milton, Qld: John Wiley & Sons Australia.

122. Borland, R. (2016). CEOS Theory: A Comprehensive Approach to

Understanding Hard to Maintain Behaviour Change. *Applied Psychology: Health and Well-Being*, 9, 3-35.

123. Clear, J. (2018). *Atomic Habits: An easy and proven way to build good habits and break bad ones*. New York: Penguin.

124. Rothman, A.J., & Salovey, P. (1997). Shaping perceptions to motivate healthy behavior: The role of message framing. *Psychological Bulletin*, 121, 3–19.

125. Akgerman, A., & Sönmez, B. (2020). The relationship between trust in first-line nurse managers and organizational commitment. *International Nursing Review*, 67(2), 183-190.

126. Breuer, C., Hüffmeier, J., Hibben, F., & Hertel, G. (2020). Trust in teams: A taxonomy of perceived trustworthiness factors and risk-taking behaviors in face-to-face and virtual teams. *Human Relations*, 73(1), 3-34.

127. McDougall, M., Ronkainen, N., Richardson, D., Littlewood, M., & Nesti, M. (2019). Three team and organisational culture myths and their consequences for sport psychology research and practice. *International Review of Sport and Exercise Psychology*, 13(1), 1-16.

128. Breuer, C., Hüffmeier, J., Hibben, F., & Hertel, G. (2020). Trust in teams: A taxonomy of perceived trustworthiness factors and risk-taking behaviors in face-to-face and virtual teams. *Human Relations*, 73(1), 3-34.

129. Australian Government Department of Finance. *The Shared Services Transformation Initiative*. https://www.finance.gov.au/government/shared-services-transformation-initiative

130. Australian Government Digital Transformation Agency. *Digital Service Platforms Strategy*. https://www.dta.gov.au/our-projects/digital-service-platforms-strategy

131. Australian Government. *Independent Review of the Australian Public Service*. https://www.apsreview.gov.au/

www.ingramcontent.com/pod-product-compliance
Lightning Source LLC
Chambersburg PA
CBHW040917210326
41597CB00030B/5110